ody
ndon

OTHER TITLES IN THIS SERIES

Royal London

bloody london

A shocking guide to
London's gruesome
past and present

Declan McHugh

crimson

First published in Great Britain in 2012 by Crimson Publishing Ltd
This reprint first published in Great Britain in 2021 by Crimson
An imprint of Hodder & Stoughton
An Hachette UK company

1

A CIP catalogue record for this title is
available from the British Library

Paperback ISBN 978 1 78059 069 1

Printed and bound in Great Britain by Clays Ltd, Elcograf S.p.A.

Hodder & Stoughton policy is to use papers that are
natural, renewable and recyclable products and made
from wood grown in sustainable forests. The logging and
manufacturing processes are expected to conform to the
environmental regulations of the country of origin.

Hodder & Stoughton Ltd
Carmelite House
50 Victoria Embankment
London EC4Y 0DZ

www.hodder.co.uk

Dedicated to the memory of my mother, Nan

CONTENTS

INTRODUCTION

In the last thirteen years I have performed my 'The Blood and Tears Walk' (**www.shockinglondon.com**) for tens of thousands of people from all over the world. The tour covers the dark side of London's history and uses a combination of detailed research and acting skills to try to create stories that are immediate, vivid, sometimes horrifying, sometimes frightening, but hopefully always interesting and real.

It is time to put some of the shocking, scary and tragic events in London's history, and the people behind those events, into book form.

This book encompasses a huge range of material ranging across the centuries – from Jack the Ripper and many other London serial killers, to execution sites, to the occult, to disasters, to prisons, to grave-robbers – and much, much more.

For each gory tale I take you to the place in question, I show you what you can see there now and, where possible, I suggest somewhere where you can soak up the atmosphere and read about the terrible events – if you dare!

I am confident that within these pages you will find stories that will inform, entertain and, yes, shock you.

I'd like to thank Crimson Publishing, and Hugh Brune in particular, for believing that I was the right person to write this book for them.

I also want to thank the three girls in my life: Ruth, and our two daughters, Bunny May Margaret, and Trixie Anna Catherine.

Declan McHugh, April 2012, London

1 WEST CENTRAL LONDON

1) Coram's Fields

93 Guilford Street, London, WC1N 1DN. The park is open all year round from 9a.m. until dusk and is free and open to children and young people under 16. Tube: Russell Square.

The Foundling Museum is at 40 Brunswick Square, London WC1N 1AZ. Tube: Russell Square. Tel: 020 7841 3600. Open Tuesday to Saturday 10a.m.-5p.m. Sunday 11a.m.-5p.m. Prices: Adult: £7.50 (£8.25 including Gift Aid), Concession: £5 (£5.50 including Gift Aid), free admission for children up to 16 years. Be sure to have a look at the statue of Thomas Coram outside the Foundling Museum. Website: www.foundlingmuseum.org.uk.

The Coram's Fields site is less than 10 minutes' walk from Russell Square tube station. Leave that tube station and cross the street. Turn right and keep walking; after a few minutes you pass a mini-roundabout and the road twists round to the right. Keep walking and at the street end turn left into Guilford Street and walk along the side of a long white building. Soon you will pass a stone structure with two pillars framing an alcove – this little alcove is the actual place in the early period of the hospital's existence which held a basket into which an unwanted child could be placed at any hour of the night. The actual entrance now for the public to enter Coram's Fields park is a small gate just a few seconds further on.

To enter the Fields themselves there is a pleasantly child-centric rule: every adult must be accompanied by a child. If you have no child with you, you can still visit the museum at 40 Brunswick Square which is back where the mini-roundabout was.

THE MAN WHO SAVED BABIES

In the early eighteenth century almost 1,000 illegitimate babies and infants were being abandoned in London each year. Dead and dying babies could be seen daily by the side of streets, either dumped by their parents (usually the mother who had been undone by a man), or left to fend for themselves. Very few were rescued.

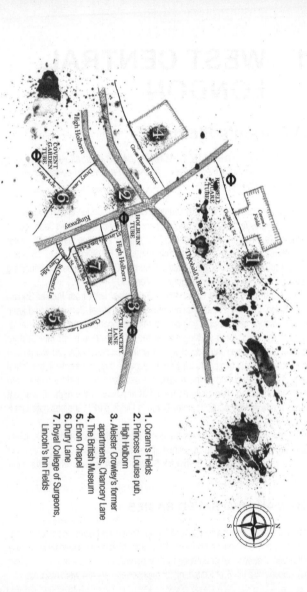

1. Coram's Fields
2. Princess Louise pub,
   High Holborn
3. Aleister Crowley's former
   apartments, Chancery Lane
4. The British Museum
5. Enon Chapel
6. Drury Lane
7. Royal College of Surgeons,
   Lincoln's Inn Fields

This infanticide was a national disgrace and one man refused to turn a blind eye to it – Thomas Coram. Thomas observed these pathetic throwaways while travelling from Rotherhithe, where he lived, to central London. It is probably not a coincidence that Coram himself had not had the happiest of childhoods. His mother had died when he was 7 and his father had sent him to sea before he was 12 years old, but he had returned triumphantly from America in 1719 a rich, self-made man.

Back in London, Coram found evidence everywhere of the abandonment of babies and was so shocked he resolved to create a 'hospital for the maintenance and education of exposed and deserted young children'.

Coram was, in effect, the Barnardo of the infants (almost 150 years later Dr Barnardo would become famous for his mission to rescue impoverished children and teenagers who were living rough in slums, on roof-tops and in all kinds of nooks and crannies in the East End).

For the next two decades after his return to England Coram campaigned to establish London's first and, for over 100 years, only home for abandoned foundling (illegitimate) children. When he was 70 years of age Coram was still tramping 10 or 15 miles a day around London seeking support and patronage for his dream. After 20 years of exhortations and constant petitioning, the home (or hospital as they called it) was finally established in 1739.

Thomas Coram could be difficult to deal with and sadly in 1742 Coram and his hospital parted ways, but plans for the hospital itself surged ahead.

Coram's vision was shared and endorsed by two other men more famous than himself – composer George Handel, and painter and satirist William Hogarth. Annual performances of Handel's *Messiah* raised the equivalent of over £500,000 in today's money for Coram's ambitious and expensive scheme. Meanwhile Hogarth (who knew plenty about child neglect – his famous print *Gin Lane* shows a toddler falling out of its drunken mother's negligent arms) set up a collection of paintings by well-known artists, the first exhibition space in Britain.

Different methods of admission were tried including 'first come, first served', balloting, and even, at one point, admitting absolutely everybody that applied. This last period lasted from 1756–1760 and is a blot on the hospital's record because granting admission to every single child led to massive overcrowding. Of the fifteen thousand children admitted only 4,300 lived to the age of 15. Also a nasty trade grew up in transporting infants to Coram's from all over the UK. Many infants died when the couriers pocketed the money and left the infants to die – a melancholy irony since the hospital was set up to avoid exactly this.

However, these sad facts have to be counterbalanced by the certainty that, particularly in the early years, many, many thousands of infants and toddlers would simply have died without Coram's intervention.

The ballot system must have been heart-rending for the unsuccessful mothers. You went into the hall and picked out a ball from a container fashioned in such a way that that there was no way of seeing what colour the ball would be. If you picked a black ball, you had to leave immediately, probably in floods of tears. If you picked a white ball your child would be admitted, subject to the formalities. Red meant you were on the reserve list.

From 1760 onwards the system changed and mothers had to petition by letters for their children to be admitted. This is the phase of the hospital's existence which is probably best known, due to the museum's permanent collection of letters written by mothers pleading for their child to be accepted. Every letter was accompanied by a unique small identifying token. This might be a drawing or a piece of fabric, in some cases just a button or even a nutshell. Knowledge of the token would be needed in case a mother's life improved to the extent that they wanted to reclaim their child. A few children were reclaimed but most children never saw their natural mothers again. Dickens (who lived opposite) borrowed the idea in *Oliver Twist* when Oliver identifies his family by means of a locket left with him.

Some of the tokens and letters are poignant in the extreme:

> *'Ann Gardiner ... born 6 October 1757 ... (her parents hope to) have her home again when they get over a little trouble they are in. She is not a bastard.'*

And Margaret Larney writes:

> *'I am the unfortunate woman that now lies under sentens of death at Newgatt (Gaol). I had a child put in here when I was sent here his name is James Larney and this one's name is John Larney ... let them know one another.'*

Foundling children were renamed and never told who their mother was, nor was the mother told the child's new name. But some mothers found out their child's identifying number and kept track of their children even when they were sent outside London for their first few years. Attending chapel these mothers would be able to surreptitiously watch their children growing up but would have no other contact.

At the age of 15, children left the Coram's Home. Most boys went into the armed forces or into apprenticeships; tailoring was also a major occupation for them. Most girls became servants. Thus the institution became known as a source of plentiful cheap labour and some unscrupulous people took advantage of that.

One such vulture was Elizabeth Brownrigg. Her brutal treatment of girls apprenticed to her, including from Coram's, culminated in murder.

You might say that by the time the institution finally closed in 1953, the childless Thomas Coram had had some 27,000 children...

The legacy continues with Coram's Fields, a large open space where children can play and where there are animals, and also with 'Coram Family', a service for vulnerable children.

2) Princess Louise pub, High Holborn

208–209 High Holborn, London, WC1V 7BW. Open Monday to Saturday 11.00a.m.-11.00p.m. Tube: Holborn.

Travel to Holborn underground station and leave by the main exit. Turn right and cross the street at the traffic lights on the left. Continue walking straight ahead into High Holborn. The Princess Louise pub is on the left-hand side and it should take you no more than 2 minutes from leaving the station to being at the pub.

NEVER LET THEM SLIP AWAY

'The end of the day, the end of the drinking, the end of a person.'

Dennis Nilsen

'I think I started off with about 15 ties. Now I've only got one left and that's a clip-on'

Dennis Nilsen

Canadian Kenneth Ockendon, a good-looking 26 year old who resembled 1970s teen idol David Cassidy, was visiting relatives in Britain at the end of 1979. On 3rd December he had been in London for two weeks. It was to be his last night.

Kenneth found himself in High Holborn near the guide-book approved lively areas of Covent Garden and Leicester Square. On the left side of High Holborn, just 2 minutes from Holborn station, stands the Princess Louise, a classic Victorian pub with 1892 décor including a horseshoe bar and lots of little screened off areas good for friendly or intimate chats. Ockendon presumably heard the jazz music playing inside and went inside to listen and have a drink or two.

In the pub Kenneth got into conversation with a Scottish 37-year-old man, a bespectacled, rather nerdish civil servant called Dennis Nilsen. In some lights Nilsen could look boyish, in other lights he looked wolfish. Nilsen happened to be a gay man who was unhappy with his sexuality and who had long been unhealthily obsessed with death. He was also already a murderer.

Nilsen knew the area well. He worked 25 minutes away at the Soho job-centre in Denmark Street, helping people find work. Nilsen paid close attention to younger male clients, particularly drifter types.

Before the job-centre Nilsen had been a policeman and he had also been a cook in the army, becoming skilled with a butcher's knife. Later Nilsen worked for a while at Dinah's Diner café in Endell Street, Covent Garden, about 7 minutes away from the Princess Louise pub (Dinah's is also still there to this day).

Nilsen was not a charismatic man, in fact he projected an aura of greyness and weariness. Conversation with him tended to be a bit one-sided since he found it hard to properly engage with other people and preferred to talk about himself in a monotone. He was something of a bore who, when drunk, could get nasty towards people he regarded as inferiors. Nilsen regarded most people as inferiors and got drunk a lot.

It is not known why exactly Ockendon went back to Nilsen's house in Melrose Avenue, Cricklewood, in north London; there is no evidence that Kenneth was gay. Perhaps to listen to music or perhaps he accepted the offer of a drink at Nilsen's house out of pity, Nilsen seeming a bit lost and lonely as Christmas fast approached. Nilsen didn't like Christmas: it reminded him that he was alone.

At Nilsen's house Kenneth was cooked for (ham, eggs and peas) then Bleep his dog watched as Nilsen strangled him to death with his headphones while Kenneth was listening to Pink Floyd.

Later Nilsen would say that it was chronic loneliness that compelled him to want to make men stay with him – permanently. In fact his first victim had been intending to leave when Nilsen had killed him on New Year's Eve 1978.

Kenneth was victim number two. In total Nilsen murdered 12 men in Cricklewood and a further three in Muswell Hill. He was eventually arrested in 1983.

In prison Nilsen busies himself with writing an autobiography already over 2,000 pages long (grandiose behaviour is a hallmark of serial killers), and attempts to get the European Court of Human Rights to take up his case for release.

FIVE LITTLE-KNOWN NILSEN FACTS

1) Nilsen appeared in the audience on Question Time in 1980. He was due to ask a question about government economic policy but was not chosen.

2) In 1970 when he was in the army, Nilsen cooked for the Queen when she visited his barracks near Balmoral.

3) Nilsen was a policeman for a year in Willesden, north-west London, where he went on to kill 12 men.

4) In 1981 Nilsen called an ambulance for an epileptic boy, Malcolm Barlow, who had collapsed feet away from his house. When the boy returned the next day after his release from hospital, Nilsen killed him.

5) Nilsen has a pitch-black sense of humour. He told a biographer that if they made a film of the murders they should introduce the cast in order of disappearance. Smoking after his confession he told a policeman who said he could just put his cigarette butts down the toilet, 'The last time I put butts down the toilet I got arrested'.

3) Location of Aleister Crowley's former apartments (now demolished)

68 Chancery Lane. Tube: Chancery Lane.

Travel to Chancery Lane underground station. Walk outside exit 4 and turn right onto High Holborn. There is at least one coffee shop around here if you want to relax and read this chapter first, or if you prefer, just 1 minute further down on the right is an excellent pub, The Cittie of Yorke. If you don't visit The Cittie of Yorke then keep walking and in another minute you will find Chancery Lane on the left. Walk into Chancery Lane and the new building at 68 Chancery Lane a few seconds in on the left is where Crowley's former apartments at 67–69 Chancery Lane used to be.

DEAD SOULS

The whole of the original building, including Crowley's apartments, was demolished in 2005 but this is where Aleister Crowley lived for about a year (1898–1899) when he was 23 years old. While workmen were knocking down the apartments in 2005 they found a human skull and pentagram in the building. This could have been some kind of sick joke, or it may well have been more sinister, but it undoubtedly scared them.

In these apartments Crowley had a white temple and a black temple (he had, at least in the beginning, an interest in white magic too). In the black temple he kept a human skeleton which he fed on dead birds and here in the apartment he claimed to have accidentally raised 316 'devils' one evening. Crowley said, 'It was the most awesome and ghastly experience I had known'.

Who was this Aleister Crowley anyway? Deep breath:

Poet. Charlatan. Novelist. Con man. Mountaineer. Drug addict. Bisexual lothario. Magician. Traveller. Painter. Iconoclast. Icon (73rd 'greatest Briton of all time' in the 2002 BBC vote). Genius (possibly). Satanist.

> *'I simply went over to Satan's side; and to this hour I cannot tell why.'*
> Crowley, Chapter 5, **Confessions**

First though, to give the devil his due, Crowley had a genius level intellect. He had amazing will-power. He was a good writer. In the beginning he was a serious seeker of what lay beyond 'the veil'. But long before the end he was, to use two of the three attributes famously applied to Lord Byron, definitely bad and dangerous to know.

He was born in 1875 to ultra-repressed parents of the Plymouth Brethren religious sect. When he was still a boy his mother told him she thought he was the devil and Crowley responded with pride, calling himself 'the Great Beast 666'. Crowley 'always disliked and despised his mother... He treated her almost as a servant'. (Crowley, Chapter Three, *Confessions*) and this almost certainly influenced his relations with women, some of whom later committed suicide. If women weren't dead souls before he met them, they certainly tended to be after he'd done with them.

Crowley travelled around the world pursuing his will and at one point he set up an HQ off Sicily in Cefalu which was the scene of intense magical ceremonies, orgies and animal sacrifices, and from which he was expelled by Mussolini. Mussolini found Crowley's activities too disturbing!

However, probably the most important thing about Crowley (and he agreed) was the 1904 publication *The Book of the Law*, a series of writings he created, although he said they were channelled by a holy guardian angel (demon?) called Aiwass. Crowley was fond of the 'SODDI' excuse – some other demon did it.

The Crowley-invented religion stemming from *The Book of The Law* is called Thelema and it still has many adherents today. Some of the sentiments sound quite romantic and almost idealistic, 'Love is the Law, Love under will' and 'Every man and every woman is a star', for example. The big problem, however, is the overarching law: 'Do what thou wilt shall be the whole of the Law'.

As I was writing this there happened to be riots and looting in London: many of the rioters would have applauded Crowley's 'Big Idea' and were in fact living it.

Supposedly you were meant to find a deeper truth within yourself before doing what you wanted to do, i.e. you were meant to concentrate hard on finding your 'True Will'; but once you had found it, moral considerations were null and void.

Crowley again:

> *'There are no "standards of Right." Ethics is balderdash. Each Star must go on its orbit. To hell with 'moral Principle;' there is no such thing; that is a herd-delusion, and makes men cattle.'*
> **The New and Old Commentaries to Liber**
> **AL vel Legis, The Book of the Law by Aleister Crowley**

Few people – basically saints and ascetics – would be able to perform such intense inner scrutiny without ego and libido getting in the way, so the commandment is an open invitation to amorality – and worse. Crowley's own life stands as a testament to the result since he left a trail of misery in his wake. Many people who fell into his orbit died badly or in strange ways.

The Hare psychopathy test is 'considered the "gold standard" for measurement of psychopathy'. Crowley passes the Hare test with flying colours. There is sometimes confusion about psychopathy; psychopaths and serial killers are not interchangeable concepts. Psychopaths are in all occupations. Quite a few businessmen and politicians, for example, who haven't killed anyone are psychopaths.

To go through some major items on the Hare check-list: Crowley was undoubtedly cunning (check) and callous (check); lacked empathy (check); was a pathological liar (check); was an egomaniac with incredibly grandiose opinions of himself (check); lacked remorse (check); was promiscuously sexual (check); was manipulative (check). In addition he had a parasitic lifestyle (check); was irresponsible (check) etc.

Crowley scores about 19 out of a possible 20 score on the Hare psychopathy test.

I also note Crowley's cruelty to animals:

> *'I therefore caught a cat, and having administered a large dose of arsenic I chloroformed it, hanged it above the gas jet, stabbed it, cut its throat, smashed its skull and, when it had been pretty thoroughly burnt, drowned it and threw it out of the window that the fall might remove the ninth life. I remember that all the time I was genuinely sorry for the animal.'*
>
> **Crowley, Chapter 6, Confessions**

Later, among other things, he crucified a toad, sacrificed pigeons for their blood and killed goats being used in magical operations at Cefalu.

There are two things that most people will find unforgiveable in Crowley despite the undoubted brilliance. One is the toadying up to the Nazis in World War Two who were certainly 'doing what they wilt' – to the crunch of broken glass and piercing screams.

Crowley, like the Nazis, despised the weak and downtrodden and fetishised the strong. Crowley's, sorry Aiwass's, feelings on the subject are worth quoting at length.

> *'We have nothing with the outcast and the unfit; let them die in their misery. For they feel not. Compassion is the vice of kings; stamp down the wretched and the weak: this is the law of the strong: this is our law and the joy of the world.'*
>
> **Crowley/Aiwass, Liber AL vel Legis, Chapter II, verse 21**

> *'... let blood flow to my name. Trample down the heathen; be upon them, O warrior, I will give you their flesh to eat. ... Sacrifice cattle, little and big; after a child ... kill and torture; spare not; be upon them!'*
>
> **Crowley/Aiwass, Liber AL vel Legis, Chapter III, verses 11, 12, 18**

Crowley hoped that the Nazis would adopt his *Book of The Law* as their New Order new bible. When the Nazis inconveniently ended up on the losing side, Crowley of course claimed that he was in fact a double agent.

Crowley made a number of extremely murky comments about human sacrifice. These murderous comments and fantasies go right back to his first writings and continue throughout his career. It is a very disturbing obsession:

> *'For the highest spiritual working one must according choose that victim which contains the greatest and purest force. A male child of perfect innocence and high intelligence is the most satisfactory and suitable victim ... But the bloody*

> *sacrifice, though more dangerous, is more efficacious: and for nearly all purposes human sacrifice is the best'.*

> **Crowley, Magick, Liber ABA, Book Four, Part III:**
> **Magick in Theory and Practice, 1912**

And in Chapter 3 of *The Book of the Law* Crowley talks about the need to sacrifice 'a child' in a particular magical ceremony. He gives the recipe for 'cakes of light' (a parody of the Eucharist) including '... rich fresh blood. The best blood is of the moon, monthly: then the fresh blood of a child, or dropping from the host of heaven: then of enemies; then of the priest or of the worshippers: last of some beast, no matter what'.

Crowley's defenders have said he was being tongue in cheek (he goes on to say he did the ritual 150 times a year for 17 years) or referring to the male sexual elixir as 'the child' but the ambivalence is deliberate since Crowley was not exactly coy normally. All these weasel words have had horrific consequences and Crowley knew what he was doing when he wrote them – he just didn't care.

Crowley's defenders also tend to ignore the following Crowley-led discussion between Crowley and his magical co-worker Victor Neuberg:

> *'The supreme Rite would be to bring about a climax in the death of the victim. By this Rite one would attain the summit of Magical Art. Even better would be to slay a girl, preferably a willing victim. After violating her, she should be cut into 9 pieces ...The Rite should not be employed on ordinary occasions, but rarely, and then for great purposes; it should not be disclosed to any man.'*

> **The Paris Working, The Book of the High Magick Art, Jan-Feb 1914**

Here are just two examples of the pernicious influence and sordid legacy of Aleister Crowley.

- In 2000 Henry Bibby, a mentally ill disciple of Crowley (who had actually gone as far as changing his name to Edward Crowley) stabbed 12-year-old Diego Pineiro-Villar to death in Covent Garden.
- In 2010 a horrifying story emerged of a Welsh child abuse circle who hero-worshipped Crowley. Members all had tattoos of Horus and the leader, Colin Batley, 'quoted from *The Book of the Law*'.

As somebody once wisely said 'By their friends ye shall know them'.

Crowley's works are undoubtedly fascinating and strangely compelling and he was extremely intelligent, but you follow him at your peril. In the end he squandered his huge gifts and went down the 'left hand path' full tilt. He was a fallen angel indeed whose last words were either (reports differ) 'I am perplexed' or 'Sometimes I hate myself'.

'I may be a Black Magician, but I'm a bloody great one' said Crowley in October 1923.

Crowley can still inspire evil as the two court cases above show, as well as the human skull the workmen found in 2005 here at this Chancery Lane location.

SOME LITTLE-KNOWN FACTS ABOUT CROWLEY
1) *Ian Fleming knew Crowley and made him the model for the bad guy, Le Chiffre, in* Casino Royale, *the first James Bond novel.*
2) *The Beatles put his picture in the collage on the cover of Sergeant Pepper.*
3) *Jimmy Page of Led Zeppelin fame is a big Crowley fan and actually bought Crowley's house in Scotland, Boleskine.*

---

4) Dr John Dee's magical items at the British Museum

Great Russell Street, London, WC1B 3DG. Tel: 020 7323 8299. Admission is free. The museum is open daily, 10a.m.–5.30p.m. The museum is closed on 1 January and 24, 25, 26 December. Tube: Russell Square or Holborn.

Walk inside the British Museum entrance and on the ground floor on the right is Room 1, The Enlightenment Galleries. Enter and turn left and look for 'Religion and Ritual, Case 20 (Magic, Mystery and Rites)'.

The glass case contains some of Dr John Dee's actual magical artefacts including an Aztec obsidian disc mirror, a crystal ball, an amulet and some inscribed wax discs.

The John Dee Society's website is at www.johndee.org.

ON HER MAJESTY'S SECRET SERVICE

It is a relief to move from Crowley to another magician, but this time one who was aiming for the light instead of plunging headlong into the darkness – Dr John Dee. Possibly *the* lost British genius (it is sad that he is totally absent from the BBC 2002 list of the top 100 Great British heroes when Aleister Crowley is in 73rd position!).

Languishing in obscurity for hundreds of years, in recent years Dee has been making a cultural comeback, with intense interest in him by assorted writers, musicians etc.

Born in Mortlake, south London on 13 July 1527, and dying 81 years later in 1608, Dee is reputedly buried in the St Mary the Virgin church in Mortlake.

Dee was a contemporary of Shakespeare although he was nearly 30 years older. The Elizabethan era was a time when London produced an unsurpassed crop of geniuses, but he was undoubtedly very special.

At that time some hugely intelligent and ambitious men were still attempting to know everything and Dee was one of them. He went to St John's College, in Cambridge, when he was just 15 and spent 16 hours a day on his studies. After St John's he went on to Cambridge's Trinity College.

Over his lifetime Dee would make important discoveries in, or contributions to, such different fields as exploration, mechanics, optics and mathematics. To quote from the British Museum website:

> *'He conceived the universe as being based on essentially magical principles, though believed that many of its rules and laws could be approached through mathematics'.*

He was also extremely knowledgeable in psychology and cryptology (code-breaking) and even found time to try to establish a national library. It seemed that whatever Dee turned his hand to he did exceedingly well and often when he was shockingly young. An overview of British writers, written when Dee was still in his twenties, already called him an 'expert astronomer'.

Dee knew many important people, from Queen Elizabeth herself down, but it is hard to escape the feeling that ultimately he was used by those in power for their own ends and in the end they abandoned him. That is what is called 'plausible deniability'.

Walsingham, the Elizabethan secret service chief used Dee's patriotism (the phrase 'the British Empire', which sounds like it has been around forever, was actually Dee's invention) and deep knowledge of secret codes.

Some of Dee's ideas sound incredibly modern. For example, Dee believed that the past and future coexisted and that there was more than one simultaneous universe. On a different level, Dee also thought it might be possible to raise lenses into the sky to focus light on Britain's enemies – he essentially foresaw the concept of the laser. He also foresaw the telescope.

Instead of a stereotypical crystal ball Dee used special polished stones for visions ('scrying') and the British Museum cabinet contains two of them: a polished stone and a black shiny disc which was originally used by the Aztecs. The larger wax disc in the British Museum cabinet is what Dee used to support the 'shew-stones'.

When he was 55 years old Dee hooked up with a 'scryer' called Edward Kelley or Kelly (Dee was honest enough to admit he couldn't scry very well by himself). Unfortunately, Dee was more other-worldly than worldly-wise and failed to notice that Kelley always wore headgear that obscured his ears. That was because earlier in his life Kelley had been found guilty of forgery and had had his ears cut off!

Kelley was actually a fraudster (unsurprisingly, Aleister Crowley in his writings identifies more with charlatan Kelley than Dee), and poor Dee even ended up being the patsy in a wife-swapping episode, engineered by Kelley, that Dee was really ashamed of.

Dee's occult interests in this era meant he was viewed with suspicion by many people who believed that the influence of witches and warlocks in human affairs was absolutely real. John Aubrey, the seventeenth-century writer said, 'in those dark times astrologer, mathematician and conjuror were accounted the same things' and indeed Dee reported that he had been called 'a companion of the Hellhounds, and a Caller, and Conjuror of wicked and damned spirits'. This was a time, after all, when errant magicians could still end up as firewood, and Dee was always walking something of a tightrope, coming very close to falling off a number of times.

He had, for example, forecast horoscopes for Queen Mary and Princess Elizabeth (as she was at the time), causing suspicion in Mary's circle which lead to Dee's temporary imprisonment in 1555, accused of enchantments and spells against Mary. Dee's own father had been ruined in Mary's reign by having held office in the previous regime and had spent a brief spell in the Tower.

However, when Elizabeth came to power she immediately adopted him as her court magician and even entrusted him with forecasting the best possible date for her coronation. Elizabeth visited him a number of times at his house in Mortlake (although she was clearly not a good picker of dates herself because when she visited Dee in 1575 she chose the day Dee was burying his wife). On another occasion, she came to his house because she wanted to see the obsidian disc mirror that is in the cabinet in the British Museum.

An example of Dee's ostensibly successful 'conversations with angels' is the 'Forest of Dean' episode. A young girl angel, Madimi, whom Dee conversed with on various subjects on various occasions, told Dee that the Forest of Dean in Gloucestershire should be watched for fire. When Dee thought about this and other cryptic pronouncements by Madimi he interpreted it to mean that perhaps

Spanish agents were planning arson attacks in the area since that particular forest was a major source of the wood used to build Elizabethan warships. The forest was searched, the agents found and the attack averted.

An example of Dee using what we would now call PsyOps (psychological operations) was his bold declaration that there would be freakishly terrible weather in 1588 and that an empire would fall (this was meant to sow seeds of doubt in Spain). In the event both forecasts came true because the Spanish Armada was destroyed by terrible weather. It is a moot point as to whether the declarations were purely political or whether Dee somehow got in touch with what the future held. Maybe a bit of both...

As previously stated, Dee was used by the high and mighty and then cast aside as times changed and he grew older. Towards the end of his life he had to suffer the indignity of a mob howling 'wizard' and burning down his library – possibly Europe's biggest – of 4,000 philosophical, scientific and arcane books.

Dee's writings are often very hard to understand. The joke about his book *The Monad*, which is notoriously difficult to make sense of, is that having presented it personally to Queen Elizabeth I, it is doubtful if she could have made head nor tail of it. Very few people can, since Dee operates at the level of a genius and does not make concessions to help comprehension.

To sum up, Dee was a polymath and deep thinker, a towering figure whose tragedy was that he was born far ahead of his time and ended up suffering the fate common to many such people (Van Gogh is another) – poverty, slander and obscurity at the time of his death.

It is well worth going to the British Museum to observe Dee's magical instruments. It makes him real and not just the protagonist in various novels that he has become.

THREE LITTLE-KNOWN FACTS ABOUT DR JOHN DEE

1) Some scholars believe that the magician Prospero in Shakespeare's The Tempest *is an amalgam of Shakespeare himself and Dr John Dee. Dee is also caricatured in the character of the alchemist Subtle in Shakespeare's rival Ben Jonson's play* The Alchemist.

2) Spy James Bond's licence to kill number '007' was first used by John Dee as his code-name while he was a spy for Queen Elizabeth I in territories now known as Germany, Russia and Czechoslovakia. '007' to Dee meant that Dee spied for Elizabeth with his two eyes (the zeroes) and the seven meant Dee considered humans to possess seven senses.

> Ian Fleming knew of Dee through Aleister Crowley who had offered his services
> to British secret sevices in World War Two when Fleming was working in British
> Intelligence. Crowley in turn had translated Dee. Fleming then borrowed 007
> for James Bond.
>
> 3) Musicians interested in John Dee include Iron Maiden who wrote a song called
> 'The Alchemist' and Damon Albarn of Blur and Gorillaz who in 2011 created a
> mini-opera based on his life.

5) Enon Chapel

St Clement's Lane, WC2A. Tube: Holborn, Temple.

The best place to read this chapter is in the George IV pub, 26–28 Portugal Street. To get there, go to Holborn tube station (Piccadilly and Central lines). After exiting the main exit, turn left into Kingsway and walk for about 10 minutes until you come to a road called Clare Market on the left. Walk to the end of Clare Market, passing St Clement's Lane on the right, and the handsome-looking George IV pub is on the left. Halfway down the short St Clement's Lane is where Enon Chapel used to be but it has entirely gone now.

In the pub a good opening gambit with a nearby student might be to tell them that (as you are about to find out) large quantities of human bones were found near here when they were preparing the site for the London School of Economics building across the way!

'DANCING ON THE DEAD'

By the early 1840s a crisis was coming to a head in London's leafy city churchyards. It had become glaringly obvious to the senses (eye and nose in particular) that these same churchyards were now full to bursting with the dead and that the continuing daily burials, amounting to 40,000 people a year, were fast turning a sad situation into an outrage and an actual threat to the health of Londoners.

The French had forbidden churchyard burials since 1804 but in London, as Charles Dickens said, 'rot and mildew and dead citizens formed the uppermost scent'.

The problem was the dramatic rise in London's population (there were close to one million more people living in London in 1840 than had been there in 1800), and the consequent increased numbers of deaths from diseases, especially cholera (see also page 44). As a result, churchyards which had once been pleasant places for quiet reflection were now becoming places of horror and the epicentres of the spread of diseases – including that same cholera.

In the 1850s emergency legislation was passed to stop any more burials in the City/central London and to speed up and develop burials in outlying cemeteries, the first of which, Kensal Green, had already opened in 1832. It was no coincidence that a cholera epidemic had hit London 6 months before Kensal Green was given the go-ahead. However, the cheapest burial at Kensal cost 30 shillings whereas Enon Chapel, the subject of this story, only charged a rock-bottom 12 shillings.

This same Enon chapel was to become notorious in the 1840s and the adverse publicity went a long way towards bringing about the much-needed change from churchyard burials to cemetery burials.

Enon chapel dated from 1822 and offered a private burial ground. Over the course of the next 22 years a minister called Howse, was responsible for the interment of around 12,000 bodies here under the chapel's wooden floor. He received 12-15 shillings per body, money which was a tidy profit and which provided a clear incentive to keep burying, come what may.

The problem Howse had was that the entire space available to him in the Enon chapel cellar was only 18 metres by 9 metres by a depth of less than 2 metres. That he somehow managed to fit 12,000 dead people into this small space was almost miraculous. Almost.

Meanwhile those living in the vicinity of the chapel were in an unenviable position. They were prone to sickness. Any meat left out went rotten in hours. People felt the taste of copper in their mouths as if they were sucking on a coin. There was a terrible smell and plagues of both rats and black flies. Yet during the entire period Howse continued to run a Sunday school for children in the chapel. The children were pestered by huge numbers of black flies, especially in summer – they called them 'body bugs'.

The hidden face of Enon was revealed when the Commissioners of Sewers inspected the vault in 1844. They were so appalled by what they found they forbade any more burials in the vault. The truth of what had actually been happening was that Howse had resorted to:

- ▪ burning the often quite expensive coffins carefully chosen by the next of kin
- ▪ using huge amounts of quicklime to destroy the lovingly deposited bodies. Quicklime would make a coffinless human body disappear in about 12 months.

With 12,000 corpses to turn into mulch, Howse must have used vast quantities of quicklime and he clearly had a total lack of respect for the dead. At one point he apparently panicked and disposed of 60 loads of earth and bones in the region of Waterloo Bridge.

Having made the discovery of the true, noxious situation beneath the floorboards, The Commissioners of Sewers bailed out and left the silent sitting tenants to rot underneath the wooden floor for 3 more years.

During those years, quite incredibly, a society of teetotallers held dances in the chapel, with just the vibrating boards they were dancing on between them and the most disgusting putrefaction. This group created a sick frisson by advertising their dances with extremely tasteless posters which played on the fact that there were dead people underneath the boards:

> *'Enon Chapel – Dancing on the Dead – Admission Threepence. No lady or gentleman admitted unless wearing shoes and stockings'.*

George Walker, a doctor, took over the building in the late 1840s and had the decency to move most of the bones to Norwood Cemetery at his own expense. Then a well-known theatrical entrepreneur took over and the place was briefly a theatre/circus space (!) before a final incarnation as 'Clare Market Chapel' in the 1890s. It was completely gone by 1914.

6) Drury Lane: first 1665 plague deaths

Drury Lane, WC2B. Tube: Covent Garden, Holborn.

A good place to read this chapter is Drury Lane Gardens. To get there go to Covent Garden underground station. Leave and turn right into Long Acre. After 5–6 minutes you will intersect with Drury Lane, turn right and walk down Drury Lane. After about 5 minutes or so you will come to Drury Lane Gardens on the right. It's open from 8a.m. until dusk.

PLAGUE CENTRAL

Today Drury Lane is an ordinary street close to the bustling Covent Garden district. It's known for the famous and grand eighteenth-century Drury Lane Theatre and an old nursery rhyme about a 'muffin man'.

In the eighteenth century, Drury Lane, despite that grand theatre, had an extremely unsavoury reputation for poverty and n'er do wells, but it is in the seventeenth century, in the year 1665 to be precise, that the words Drury Lane struck real terror into people because of a strange and new phenomenon – red crosses marking certain doors in the street. Here is where the 1665 London plague effectively began.

> *'This day, much against my will, I did in Drury Lane see two or three houses marked with a red cross upon the doors, and "Lord have mercy upon us" writ there – which was a sad sight to me, being the first of that kind that to my remembrance I ever saw.'*
>
> **Samuel Pepys, 7 June 1665**

The plague was back.

Largely gone for a couple of generations it had now returned with a virulence so horrifying that it could only be compared to the Black Death of 1348 over 300 years before.

People forcibly shut up in the houses chalked with red crosses faced a terrifying ordeal. They were not allowed out until 40 days had passed ('quaranta', hence quarantine) and if anyone became newly ill with plague during that time another 40 days was added. During those interminable days they were cooped up in claustrophobic conditions with their loved ones and/or lodgers – but usually with seriously ill and infectious loved ones or lodgers. No wonder that some people tried to escape the dreadful nightmare by throwing themselves from windows, even at the cost of death or serious injury. Others went mad. Others tried to save their babies by bribing the watchman and passing them from windows.

At its worst (the third week in September 1665 saw record numbers of deaths), the plague caused an almost total breakdown of society. Samuel Pepys wrote in his diary on 1 October 1665, 'Things here must break in pieces'.

Many rich people (including the King) just took off for the country or plague-free towns, leaving the desperate masses behind. Paranoia was everywhere. A spot would be noted by both its bearer and others. A cough could cause instant silence. If someone did cough or sneeze, you automatically said 'Bless you' because the sneezer might just have shown a sign of plague. 'Bless you' had, of course, an undercurrent of 'God help me'.

The Parish of St Giles Cripplegate, close to where the Barbican Arts Centre is today, was perhaps worst hit by the plague. In 1665, 3,200 people died from 2,000 households in that Cripplegate district alone. It has been suggested that the stinking ditch there at the time (it was just outside the London Wall) could have been partly responsible for this enormous number of deaths from just one parish.

London was a large city normally full of noise and hustle and bustle. Now, apart from the moans or screams of those dying in intolerable pain, it became almost a silent city with practically deserted streets overgrown with weeds.

People tried not to go out unless they had to because they feared meeting an infected person who might lurch at them, so people who did venture out would do strange zigzag walking movements in the streets. On the other hand, people were also afraid to stay inside all the time in cramped conditions with others, any one of whom might have the plague secretly developing in his or her body. The situation is strongly reminiscent of modern 'zombie' films as you can see from this quote from Samuel Pepys on 16 October 1665, 'But Lord, how empty the streets are, and melancholy, so many poor sick people in the streets, full of sores'. Could the genesis of modern zombie films lie in the folk memories of those seventeenth-century nightmare days and nights?

Pepys again, on 12 August 1665:

> *'The people die so, that now it seems they are fain to carry the dead to be buried by daylight, the nights not sufficing to do it in. And my Lord Mayor commands people to be within at 9 at night ... that the sick may have liberty to go abroad for ayre.'*

Despair ruled. A contemporary illustration shows a skeleton frenziedly shaking its bony arms with coffins strewn all around, and at the top the words 'Lord, have mercy on London'.

This was a time which revealed both the best and the worst of human behaviour. Some magnificently courageous people, including some priests and ministers, some doctors and the Lord Mayor (who could easily have found an excuse to leave London but didn't) put themselves in harm's way repeatedly and yet some survived.

On the other hand, the plague brought out the worst side of human nature in some other people. 'Searchers', for example, carried white wands and were usually old women paid five to eight shillings a week to visit plague houses and check whether inhabitants were sick of plague or other diseases, and then to report the results back to the surgeons. They were notoriously mercenary and unfeeling, often drunk, and many would basically rob the stricken inhabitants of plague houses. They were also open to bribes to avoid a house being quarantined. Some of them were accused of murder. The Reverend Thomas Vincent said that the plague victims feared the nurse more than the plague itself.

Then there were the body collectors: a notorious crew, on ten shillings a week, who would shout 'bring out your dead'. Perhaps you had to be a little bit mad to do such work or perhaps such work made you mad. Some people did it to steal from the bodies. One in particular was infamous (maybe he was crazed) for his brutality. Grinning he would seize the corpses and even manhandle – and worse – the female ones.

At the end, when the plague rage ebbed away in the spring and summer of 1666, approximately 110,000 London inhabitants had died out of a population of about 260,000. This is very approximately about the same proportion of deaths in the population as had been killed by the fourteenth-century Black Death.

What was the 1665 plague exactly? Nearly 350 years later it is still not certain, and a crop of researchers is radically challenging former ideas about its origin and identity.

The fourteenth-century Black Death is also controversial and a hotbed of debate, but very recent research into bacterium DNA from the teeth of Black Death plague victims buried near the Tower of London means that those proposing that the Black Death was bubonic plague, caused by the bacterium Yersinia pestis, again have the upper hand.

The 1665 plague however is a different matter. The 'rat with fleas' model of the origins of the 1665 plague is under serious threat. A growing number of researchers are pointing out problems with that theory. One problem is that there was no big increase in rats seen before the plague struck in 1665. This is odd. Scientific papers are now being written, and treated with increasing respect, that suggest that although the Black Death may well have been caused by bubonic plague, the 1665 plague might have been a virus and not bubonic plague, or that it was a combination of diseases.

THREE URBAN MYTHS ABOUT THE PLAGUE
URBAN MYTH ONE
Assertion: *The Great Fire of 1666 destroyed any plague lingering from 1665.*
Reality: *This is simply not true. The area that the Great Fire consumed was largely in the City area, the oldest part of London, while the great majority of plague victims the year before had been living in the area outside the city walls.*

URBAN MYTH TWO
Assertion: *The Piccadilly line (or the Central line – the myth varies) curves at certain points to avoid plague pits.*
Reality: *Plague pits were not dug very deep. With thousands dying every week there was simply no time and there was also no mechanical equipment. The London Underground system (certainly in the case of those two lines) was dug much deeper than this and there would therefore have been no contact between plague pits and those tube trains.*

URBAN MYTH THREE

Assertion: *The 'Ring a ring o' roses' nursery rhyme is actually referring to plague and its effects such as sneezing and finally falling down dead.*

Reality: *This so-called 'plague' nursery rhyme was not known in its current form until the late nineteenth century although it has resemblances to similar rhymes before then, including in other countries. The problem for those who assert the plague meaning is that the earlier rhymes, which are more likely to be closer to the original rhyme, do not have words that support the plague interpretation and it was not until after World War Two that the plague idea occurred to people.*

7) Royal College of Surgeons, Hunterian Collection

35-43 Lincoln's Inn Fields, London, WC2A 3PE. Tel: 020 7869 6560. Open Tuesday to Saturday 10a.m.–5p.m. Admission is free and the museum is open to all. Free curator's tour every Wednesday at 1p.m. If you have a group of over 10 individuals please ring in advance. Tube: Holborn.

To get to the Hunterian Collection of the Royal College of Surgeons travel to Holborn underground station. Walk outside the main exit of the station and turn left. Immediately on the left is a narrow street called Gate Street, walk down it. In a few seconds you will see The Ship pub on the left; at that point turn sharp right and you will shortly find a park on the left-hand side called Lincoln's Inn Fields. Don't turn left just keep walking ahead of you down the edge of that park and in a few minutes when the park ends turn left into the south side of Lincoln's Inn Fields and you will find the Royal College of Surgeons, a white building with huge pillars, on the right-hand side.

VERY SPECIAL PEOPLE

This collection is *not* intended as a horror attraction or a Ripleys-esque freak-show. It is a free collection primarily meant for people in the medical profession, but respectful members of the public can go.

The three individuals written about in this chapter had unfortunate lives and it's good to keep in mind when observing them that any one of us could have suffered similar kinks in DNA.

EXHIBIT ONE
The Irish Giant. Case 8.

Charles Byrne, who sometimes went by the show name O'Brien, was a 7 foot 8 inch (2.33 metres) tall Irish giant whose skeleton is on display here.

Nowadays we know that such gigantism is often caused by pituitary gland disorders which can lead to a condition called acromegaly characterised by abnormally long limbs and large facial features. Doctors have confirmed, after examination of the pituitary region of his skull, that Byrne did indeed have such a pituitary condition.

Byrne was born in 1761 and came to London when he was 21 to make his fortune. Like the Elephant Man in the nineteenth century, he made a living by allowing himself to be gawped at by thrill-seeking crowds. He even got to meet King George III. In fact there were two Irish giants roaming the country at the same time since Byrne had a huge rival, Patrick Cotter, who was even bigger but perhaps not as good at publicising himself.

Byrne turned to alcohol abuse, no doubt exacerbated by the anguish caused by doctors telling him to his face that they would body-snatch him after his death. An amazing physical specimen such as his body would be worth a fortune in a museum or collection or show. One night while drunk he had all his life's savings stolen and it was the final straw. Feeling death's approach, he made plans to be buried at sea, away from the depredations of rapacious surgeons. John Hunter however, the anatomist who founded this Hunterian Collection, paid the astonishing amount of £500 (around £30,000 in today's money) to the undertaker for his corpse. Hunter then boiled up the corpse in a huge pot in his family house, stripped off the flesh, and installed the skeleton (discoloured by the boiling) in the Hunterian Collection where it remains today.

Genetic research into Byrne and some other genuine Irish giants indicates that there was a common ancestor some 1,500 years ago. This may be a factor in the frequency of the occurrence of giants in Irish mythology. In one of those very strange coincidences that make you wonder, Byrne was born just a few miles away from Lough Neagh, a lake which has featured for centuries — long before Byrne was born — in one of the Irish giant myths. In that myth, giant Fionn mac Cumhaill (pronounced Fin McCool) created Lough Neagh by hurling some land at a Scottish giant. He missed, and the earth landing in the sea formed the Isle of Man while the hole left behind filled with water to become Lough Neagh.

EXHIBIT TWO
The Sicilian little person. Case 14, Bay 6.

Caroline Crachami's skeleton is in the Hunterian Collection too. Crachami is Byrne's complete opposite being a very little person 19.8 inches tall (50.5 cm). She was supposed to have been born in Palermo in 1815 and was known as the Sicilian dwarf. Like Byrne, while she was being exhibited in London she too met the reigning king of her time, in her case George IV. She had been exhibited at Smithfield's Bartholomew Fair and described there under the heading of 'A CHANGELING CHILD' as:

> 'a Fairy Child ... not exceeding a foot and a half high ... seems so grave and solid, as if it were Threescore Years old. You may see the whole anatomy of its body by setting it against the Sun. It never speaks. It has no teeth, but is the most voracious and hungry creature in the world'.

There is doubt about her real age and although it had been thought that she had died when she was about nine years old, recent research on her teeth indicates that she may actually only have been about three years old when she died, but had a condition which made her look wizened and old. The painting near her skeleton shows her looking like a little old lady. If she had in fact been nearer three years old it would explain why she could only say a few babyish words. She probably died of tuberculosis and may have suffered from a genetic condition called 'Seckel syndrome'. After her death, the showman who had been exhibiting her attempted to sell the body to anatomy schools but she ended up in Hunter's Collection. The child's father turned up to retrieve Caroline's body only to find dissection was already underway and he went away again in extreme distress.

EXHIBIT THREE
The double-headed Bengali child skull. Crystal Gallery, Bay 110, Shelf 2.

This boy's skull – or skulls – is both amazing and disturbing. The name of the child concerned is unknown but he was born in Bengal in 1783 and lived for about 4 years with two skulls and two faces fused together on top of one another. The upper skull faces backwards. The two different heads did not synchronise emotions and possibly the movements of the features of the upper head were reflex only. Apparently the eyes in the upper face never shut, even at night, but kept constantly moving, even when the normal head was asleep, and the upper mouth salivated when the lower mouth was fed. The child, it is said, had been thrown by the horrified midwife into the fire after its birth but was rescued, although with an injured eye and ear. The parents exhibited their child for money during its life but he is said to have died from a cobra bite aged 4.

The man who founded the Hunterian Collection, collector/anatomist/ consorter with grave-robbers, John Hunter, embodied some of the best and some of the worst aspects of the new eighteenth-century scientific attitude. His thirst for knowledge was tremendous and was allied to his huge capacity for hard work. However rationality tended to overpower emotion and empathy. Clearly the pursuit by Hunter (and others) of giant Charles Byrne caused Byrne real distress. Also animals suffered badly at Hunter's hands. He conducted some exceedingly weird experiments such as implanting a tooth in a cockerel's head (the result is to be seen in the Collection), and multitudes of other animal experiments. He was a bit of a Dr Moreau. In his defence he also experimented on himself and, for example, infected himself with syphilis so he could rigorously observe its effects.

We now live in a time where reparations are made for cultural insensitivity, including scientific insensitivity. Aboriginal remains have been returned to Australia and Native American remains have been returned to the United States.

We know that Byrne wanted to be buried in the ground but strongly suspected that he would be grave-robbed, hence his desperate plan to be buried at sea as the second-best option. Is it perhaps time to accede to Byrne's wish, brazenly thwarted by Hunter, remove him from the glass case where he continues to be gazed on after death as he was throughout his life, and bury him in the ground in Ireland where other members of his family lie?

1) On 10 May 1941 a World War Two bomb led to the loss of thousands of the exhibits in the Hunterian Collection. They were strewn all over the street outside the building, leading to the bizarre spectacle of pickled body parts being taken away on stretchers.

2) In 1998 42-year-old Anthony-Noel Kelly, a butcher turned artist, was jailed for 9 months for macabre activities connected to the Royal College of Surgeons. Kelly had always been 'obsessed with death' (his words) and had been given permission by the College to sketch body parts there. Instead he paid a lab technician £400 to smuggle out actual body parts from over 40 human bodies. The grisly haul was wrapped in black bin liners which were then placed in a rucksack and taken on London Underground trains to Kelly's studio. This went on for over a year. Kelly made moulds of the parts, including human heads, and mounted

an exhibition. The Inspector of Anatomy attended the exhibition and called in the police who discovered two heads, legs and a torso at a flat and buried in a field. Feebly, Kelly retaliated that the College had been keeping the body parts in 'an unattractive way' and that he had 'buried them with dignity'. Jailing Kelly, the judge disagreed and called it 'a revolting theft'. Kelly later described the police as having 'raped' his studio.

This case made legal history as it established that human body parts were capable of being property if 'they have acquired different attributes by virtue of the application of skill, such as dissection or preservation techniques, for exhibition or teaching purposes'.

THREE MORE LONDON EXECUTION SITES

Charing Cross

Until 1660 if you had stood where the National Gallery is now and looked down on what is now Trafalgar Square there would have been no Nelson's Column in front of you (it wasn't completed until 1844), but you would have seen a gallows close to where the Column is today. Many people died here over the years for a variety of crimes ranging from pickpocketing to murder.

The most famous people hanged here were the so-called 'regicides': people who had been involved in putting King Charles I to death. Thirteen of them were deliberately executed here because it was just a short walk away from where Charles I had himself been executed at Whitehall in 1649. The spot where the regicides were executed is where the statue of Charles I on horseback is today.

Thomas Harrison was the first of the unlucky 13 and went to his death, says Samuel Pepys, 'as cheerfully as any man could in that condition' ie about to be hung, drawn and quartered. Harrison in one account is supposed to have given his executioner 'a box on the ear' when they cut into his body to quarter him. They made sure to hang Harrison looking towards the Banqueting House where Charles I had died.

It shows how jaded Pepys was by the frequency of executions in his day that after the quote about Harrison he immediately goes on to talk about some oysters he gave to some friends later that same day.

Lincoln's Inn Fields

In 1586 Anthony Babington and 13 other malcontents plotted to kill Queen Elizabeth I and replace her with Mary, Queen of Scots. The queen's spy-master, Walsingham, found out about the plot and Babington and the rest were sentenced to be hung, drawn and quartered as traitors. Lincolns Inn Fields was chosen because Babington's house had been round the corner at Holborn and the plot had been hatched in the area.

The executions took place where the little bandstand is today in the centre of the Fields. Seven of the conspirators were to be executed on the first day, and the remaining seven on the second day. In the event it was a rare example in London's history of when a hostile, execution-hardened crowd who had flocked here precisely because they wanted to see men put to death by hanging, drawing and quartering, rebelled. The crowd became sickened by the sadistic prolonging of the process and began to murmur, and appeared restless and potentially mutinous. Queen Elizabeth I herself was informed and on the second day the remaining seven conspirators were allowed to be hanged until they were dead first, before the mutilations began.

Wapping

From the sixteenth century, Wapping, by the Thames in east London, is known as the execution site where pirates kicked their heels. The Captain Kidd pub today is close to where the executions would have taken place.

The procedure was that the pirate, or other criminal guilty of crimes at sea, was taken here by cart from Newgate. A silver oar accompanied the prisoner as the symbol of authority and the cart contained the prisoner's own coffin too. After the hanging the body was slung into the coffin and sometimes then, in what was for some prisoners a fate worse than death, taken off to the Surgeons' Hall where its dissection was a matter of public display. After being hacked at by various surgeons and students for up to a week in public, the body, much the worse for wear, was brought back here to Wapping to be rehanged in chains for carrion birds to peck at. Hanging bodies were left 'until three tides have overflowed them'.

When notorious pirate-catcher turned pirate himself, Captain Kidd, died here in 1701 the first attempt at his execution failed because the rope broke and he fell to the ground. There was no reprieve though, the still conscious Kidd was hauled back up and, in a nifty bit of improvisation, pushed from a ladder leaning against the gallows and so rehanged. Kidd's tarred body was to be seen, hung in chains, for the next two years at the mouth of the Thames Estuary.

2 WEST LONDON

1) The Cato Street conspirators

Tube: Edgware Road.

Remarkably, The actual former cow and horse stable, where the conspirators met prior to attempting to behead every member of the Cabinet, is still in Cato Street with an official blue plaque on it.

To get here, go to Edgware Road station using the Circle/District/ Hammersmith & City lines (because the Bakerloo line station is an entirely separate building some 150 yards away). Turn left out of the station. Walk to the top of the road you are on, called Chapel Street, and at the top opposite on the right is a street called Homer Street. Walk down Homer Street, at the end turn right into Crawford Street past the Larrik pub on the left and into Crawford Place. One minute later you come to Cato Street on the left which you enter through a white-bricked archway. The actual building with its plaque does not have a number on its door so it presumably belongs to the building immediately to the left which is No. 1 Cato Street.

If you want a quiet place to read this chapter, just across the road from Cato Street is the Windsor Castle pub and there is the aforemential The Larrik.

REVOLUTION IN A COWSHED

Arthur Thistlewood, James Ings, Thomas Brunt, Richard Tidd and William Davidson and others plot to behead the entire Cabinet.

In 1820, revolution was in the air in Europe, and England was not immune from the feeling that 'the times they were a-changin'. The Battle of Waterloo had been won in 1815 but with a huge cost to the country as soldiers flooded back home. Many had been injured and had become rudely disillusioned at the lack of rehabilitation, and indeed their general treatment. In addition, the passage of the first of the Corn Laws that same year meant that farmers were protected but poor people had to pay artificially high prices for corn and other grains. The cost of living rocketed and wages were depressed. The Manchester Peterloo massacre in 1819, when soldiers attacked a working-class meeting demanding the reform of parliament leaving 11 dead and 400 injured, radicalised thousands.

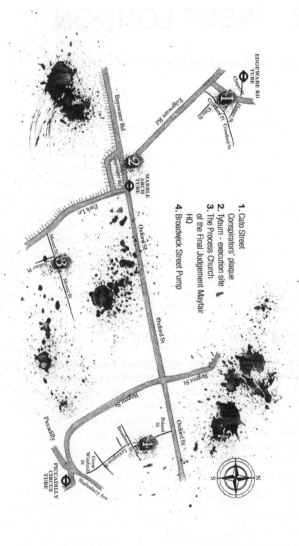

1. Cato Street
Conspirators' plaque
2. Tyburn - execution site
3. The Process Church
of the Final Judgement Mayfair
HQ
4. Broadwick Street Pump

EDGEWARE RD
TUBE

Bayswater Rd

Edgeware Rd

Chapel St

Homer St

Crawford Pl Crawford St

Cato St

MARBLE
ARCH
TUBE

Oxford St

Park Ln

Mount St

Balfour Pl

Mount St

Oxford St

Regent St

Oxford St

Poland St

Broadwick St

Great
Windmill St

PICCADILLY
CIRCUS
TUBE

Piccadilly

Shaftesbury Ave

Then, in January 1820 King George III finally died and a newspaper revealed that the entire Cabinet was due to have a meal together in Grosvenor Square, close to Marble Arch.

All of this was the crucible from which the Cato Street conspiracy emerged.

The leader of the conspiracy was Arthur Thistlewood, and the four other main protagonists were Ings, Brunt, Tidd and Davidson. It was a working-class assembly of carpenters, butchers, shoemakers, tailors, etc.

There are parallels with the Guy Fawkes plot to kill King James and others at the state opening of parliament in 1605, not least because both groups of conspirators had been infiltrated by spies and both governments knew of the plots against them but played along to try to catch the conspirators red-handed.

It was Arthur Thistlewood's right-hand man, George Edwards, who first suggested the wholesale murder of the Cabinet as he pointed out the newspaper item about the meal the ministers were going to have in Grosvenor Square. In fact no such meal had been planned and the newspaper item had been deliberately fabricated and then inserted in the newspaper precisely to entrap the would-be assassins. The whole thing was a set-up and Edwards was a government agent, one of many spies and informers who had infiltrated the numerous radical groups at the time.

Although their fate was to be gruesome, no romance should be attached to the conspirators. This was not going to be some kind of noble 'velvet revolution', but rather a botched-up semi-farcical attempt at mass murder by desperate men. They had been energised by the spirit of revolution in the air and extreme poverty also played its part. They were so poor that they could not afford a light or more than two chairs for the planning meetings; at times they could barely speak due to hunger. As Ings said later when asked why he had conspired, 'I could not keep [ie provide for] my wife and children.'

Thistlewood was a well-known radical face about town who had actually been charged with high treason just 3 years before the Cato Street meeting but had been acquitted precisely because the jury disliked the element of entrapment in that case. With two attempts at high treason in three years you could say that Thistlewood was a man on a mission.

Ings had a wife and four children. All his attempts at business had failed and he was bitter and desperate. He told the others that he wanted to personally behead every member of the Cabinet once they were trapped and confronted. He even had plans to display two particular members' heads on Westminster Bridge after first showing them around some poor districts. In the end heads did indeed get shown, but they included Ings' own and did not belong to any Cabinet ministers.

Brunt was possibly the most hot-headed and impatient of the conspirators; he proposed at a planning meeting that if anyone failed to do what he was supposed to do during the attack on the ministers, he should be 'run through on the spot', and as he was about to die he shouted that military government would continue In England unless there were many more men like them.

Davidson was a man of colour (his words) from Jamaica who was one of those who had been radicalised by the Manchester Peterloo Massacre.

Tidd, aged about 45, looked as if he was the oldest member of the conspirators although Thistlewood was actually older. He had for many years dreamed that he would end up on the gallows.

These were all men who might have said, as one of the murderers in Shakespeare's *Macbeth* says:

'I am one…
Whom the vile blows and buffets of the world
Have so incensed that I am reckless what
I do to spite the world.'

On 23 February 1820 the 25 to 30-strong gang, bristling with weapons of all sorts, met in the Cato Street stable building – not far from where the fictitious cabinet meal was meant to be held – to make final preparations for their violent attack. The stable was raided by the Bow Street Runners, the famous Covent Garden-based pre-Metropolitan Police force. The Runners were well aware of the gang's intentions because of George Edwards and other informers.

A contingent of soldiers who were meant to back the police up arrived ever so slightly late for the action, having got lost. This was the first of a number of almost slapstick elements in the scene that ensued as guns failed to fire or missed at impossibly close quarters, while people grappled with each other in the hay or slipped over dunghills. The sword through his guts that policeman Richard Smithers received, killing him, was no joke though. Thistlewood had murdered Smithers and managed to escape but he was soon recaptured.

For the crime of high treason the punishment was to be hung, drawn and quartered but, in the event, once (inevitably) found guilty at their Old Bailey trials, the five were just hung and posthumously decapitated. The full penalty was not exacted because the times had moved on from the butcheries of the Elizabethan era at places such as Smithfield (see page 99), plus the authorities were well aware that some people had a degree of sympathy for the conspirators' actions.

They were 'inevitably' found guilty because chief provocateur Edwards played no part in the trial so no awkward questions about entrapment could be asked of him. Instead a few of the minor-league conspirators were pressurised to give evidence against the leaders in return for softer sentences.

William Davidson said at the trial:

> *'It is an ancient custom to resist tyranny ... And our history goes on further to say, that when another of their Majesties the Kings of England tried to infringe upon those rights, the people armed, and told him that if he did not give them the privileges of Englishmen, they would compel him by the point of the sword ... Would you not rather govern a country of spirited men, than cowards? ... I can die but once in this world, and the only regret left is, that I have a large family of small children, and when I think of that, it unmans me.'*
>
> **The whole proceedings on the Trial of William Davidson and Richard Tidd, for High Treason ... , 1820**

Although he was cold-blooded, there is no doubting Thistlewood's bravery. When sentence of death was passed on him he timed it so that he took snuff at that exact moment (an equivalent gesture today would be for him to have popped some chewing gum into his mouth).

The executions took place at Newgate on 1 May 1820.

Thistlewood's coolness/cold-bloodedness, persisted all the way to the scaffold and right up to the moment of his death. When he appeared on the scaffold he said, 'I never felt in better spirits all my life'. He might even have been telling the truth, since life had given him little. Such apparent unconcern in the face of death was appreciated by the huge execution crowd of some 80,000 people (although large, that was by no means the largest crowd ever seen at the Newgate execution site.) Such crowds tend to despise whingers, backsliders and tremblers and Thistlewood in particular was none of those. Davidson, on the other hand, turned to religion at the last.

The decapitations, ritually performed, were macabre in the extreme and shocked the crowd. Once all five men had been hanging for 30 minutes and so were undoubtedly dead, a sinister masked man – never definitely identified – knelt by the side of the coffin in which Thistlewood's body had been placed. Thistlewood's head was then held over the edge of the coffin and cut off by the masked man with an extremely sharp knife, This process took about one minute and about four cuts. Thistlewood's head was then held up by an assistant and the masked man said, 'This is the head of Arthur Thistlewood – a traitor', which roused some members of the crowd to boo and hiss. The process was then repeated with each of the other four men. The decapitations after death of the Cato Street five were the last in British execution history.

The bodies of the conspirators were later dumped into lime in Birdcage Walk, also known as Deadman's Walk, a dank and uneven stretch of burial ground within Newgate prison. It had an iron grille above (hence the ironic appellation 'birdcage'), and prisoners were forced to walk down its length on their way to and from court.

Photographs exist which show the initial letters of the Cato Street conspirators' surnames here: T I B D T. Only initial letters of surnames were painted on the walls at Birdcage Walk, to afford the executed as little dignity as possible. That one letter, however, would still let other prisoners know who was referred to and the prisoners still living would be forced to think on their fate, and the fate of others like them, as they walked over the ground where the bones lay.

Although there is no definite proof, several different contemporary sources give the name of the masked decapitator as Tom Parker. Parker was a thuggish resurrectionist (the preferred euphemistic term used by grave-robbers themselves), who used to boast he had snatched 14 bodies from Old St Pancras graveyard (see page 56). Such a person would certainly be familiar with decapitation (to obtain teeth which were sold for money to denture-makers). Parker never admitted it, but he also never denied it.

FOUR OTHER ASSASSINATION ATTEMPTS IN LONDON

1) There were seven unsuccessful attempts on the life of Queen Victoria over a period of 42 years by Messrs Oxford, Francis, Bean, Hamilton, Pate, O'Connor and, finally, McLean. Four were transported, one went to prison, and two were acquitted but detained in insane asylums. In all the attempts it seems that only two actual bullets were fired, the rest either had no bullet in their gun, or only powder, and one had tobacco! The only actual injury wasn't caused by a gun but by Pate with a walking stick.

2) In 1812 the then Prime Minister, Spencer Perceval, was shot dead in the lobby of the House of Commons by John Bellingham. Bellingham was an embittered merchant who got into debt in Russia and blamed the government – so on his return to England he killed the head of that government. The government rushed through his hanging just one week later in case he was part of some kind of plot rather than an individual acting alone.

3) In 1978 Georgi Markov, a Bulgarian dissident writer, was waiting by a bus-stop on Waterloo Bridge when someone 'accidentally' stabbed him in the

> back of his right leg, possibly with the tip of an umbrella because when Markov looked down a man was retrieving one from the ground. This man, who had a foreign accent, got into a taxi and left the scene in a hurry. Whatever the mechanism was that propelled a pin-head sized pellet of the deadly poison Ricin into Markov's leg, it caused him to die four days later of blood poisoning.
>
> A former Russian KGB general, Oleg Kalugin, subsequently openly admitted that the KGB and the Bulgarian Secret Service carried out the assassination between them.
>
> It's little consolation to any of Markov's friends or family, but Time magazine rated this the fifth top assassination plot of all time.
>
> 4) In 1973, as his first action in a long and bloody terrorist career, Ilich Ramirez Sanchez (better known as Carlos 'The Jackal'), attempted to murder Edward Sieff, the Jewish chairman of the Marks and Spencer department store. Carlos went to Sieff's house in the St John's Wood district in west London and forced the butler to take him to Sieff whom he then shot in the face. The gun then jammed before he could fire again and the Jackal had to run off. Sieff survived.

2) Tyburn

Tube: Marble Arch.

Travel to Marble Arch underground station, leave the station at exit 1 and walk to the right. You are on the road called Marble Arch and you soon come to the intersection of two large, busy and grimy London roads (Marble Arch itself and Edgware Road on the right). Either stand here or visit the Tyburn pub just 60 seconds up Edgware Road on the right-hand side.

THE 600 YEAR LONG HORROR SHOW

If you stand at the junction of the two roads amid the noisy traffic, with thousands of people coming and going around you, there will be very little to alert you to the fact that you are standing at the absolutely grimmest site in London's history. Cumulatively, there have been more violent deaths here than anywhere else in London's history. This was London's Golgotha …

If you look closely you can spot an easily-missed and underwhelming little plaque in the pavement 'island' at the beginning of Edgware Road. The circular stone marking says 'The Site of Tyburn Tree' and it has a cross in the middle. This area was formerly known as Tyburn because of an underground river here of that name, but there was nothing pleasant or leafy about the tree because it referred to the wooden gallows or hanging 'tree' also known as 'the deadly never green' or 'the fatal tree'.

Here then is the stored up psychic horror of 600 years' worth of judicial executions. It is calculated that some 50–60,000 people were executed near the spot where the plaque is, from 1196 when William 'Longbeard' Fitzosbert was hanged for a tax rebellion, until 1783 when John Austen was the last person to hang at the site.

In the first part of Tyburn's history a single long beam was used which could accommodate up to 10 people hanging at the same time. By 1571 the classic structure was in place: a flat triangle of three thick wooden beams, on three 18 feet high posts. Eight people could be hanged on each of the three sides, twenty-four in total. This three-sided permanent gallows was in place for nearly 200 years before a mobile hanging platform was substituted.

Hanging was the method but not the long-drop method that killed John Haigh (see page 135) for example. Instead the short-drop method was used which meant a slow death by strangulation rather than having your neck broken. You would limp towards death for 20 minutes or so, longer if you were unlucky. Twentieth-century state executioner Albert Pierrepoint described this method of killing, in a pithy and accurate phrase, as 'batch-strangulation in public'.

In 1783 the execution site was switched to Newgate prison, largely because wealthy locals had successfully protested at the large numbers of unsavoury characters congregating close to their mansions on execution days.

In The Tyburn pub or even just on the street by the plaque, I would encourage you to think for a few minutes about the 60,000 hanged and the accumulated horror experienced by all those who died here, not to mention their families and friends.

Imagine what it would be like to actually be someone preparing to be executed at Tyburn. The disbelief that it could actually be happening to you. The torturing regrets. The extra horror (worse than the hanging itself said some of the condemned) of being stared at by scores of thousands for a couple of hours as the death cart proceeds from Newgate prison along the 3 mile (5 km) route of the modern day Oxford Street. Imagine being forced to observe the jam-packed spectators, each of them feeling just a little bit more alive themselves as they watch your white, pinched face on the last day of your life. The dread reminder of the coffin travelling with you. Then the horror-show at the execution site itself with raucous crowds numbering anything up to 200,000 filching, fighting and fornicating, as well as swearing, laughing, and heckling. Finally, you see through the alcoholic haze created by the drink mercifully given to you en route to try to numb reality, the hangman, himself drunk. The knowledge that this man will take your clothes after your death as a perk of the job and later sell the rope you dangle from, gasping for breath as you slowly suffocate, for so many pence per inch in local bars. Also the knowledge that your corpse might well be man-handled after your death by people who believed that touching a hanged man or woman could bring benefits to heath and fortune. Noose round your neck now, the cart moves off followed by merciful oblivion – but not for 20 minutes.

A pamphlet of 1784 (the year after the last execution at Tyburn) succinctly summed up all that had been wrong with a process originally meant to frighten people into more moral lifestyles. Instead of reverent and moral thoughts the atmosphere at Tyburn had in fact become that of a public holiday. Huge crowds encouraged crime and many crimes were committed at the execution-site itself including, of course, pickpocketing. As the pamphlet pointed out:

> *'When (people) view the meanness of the apparatus, the dirty cart and ragged harness, surrounded by a sordid assemblage of the lowest among the vulgar, their sentiments are inclined more to ridicule than pity'.*

In fact anyone manifesting piety in their last minutes was jeered at whereas swaggerers who had reconciled themselves to receiving a 'wry neck and wet trousers' were cheered.

It is perhaps ironic that former British Prime Minister Tony Blair has bought a house literally metres from where Tyburn Gallows stood. Sweet dreams, Tony!

TWO SCENES FROM TYBURN'S HISTORY

HANNAH DAGOE

James Boswell, Samuel Johnson's friend and biographer, saw Hannah Dagoe at Newgate shortly before her death and was not impressed by her, but in 1763 she put on one of the greatest 'shows' Tyburn ever saw. Tyburn crowds wanted entertainment and they loved a criminal who didn't break down at the last moment and Hannah gave them both. Irish Hannah, who had been sentenced to death for burglary and robbery, managed to get her hands free on the journey along what is now Oxford Street, and told the hangman she dared him to hang her before proceeding to punch him so hard that he nearly fell out of the execution cart. Clearly very much disliking her appointed executioner she then decided to prevent him from selling her clothes after her death by stripping completely naked and hurling the clothes into the crowd. Then she did her best not to let him get the noose round her neck and when he finally managed to do so, she instantly hurled herself out of the cart breaking both the rope and her neck.

Hannah certainly did not 'go gentle into that dark night!'; 'rage, rage against the dying of the light' was more her style.

WILLIAM DUELL

William Duell was a nasty piece of work who had robbed and murdered his victim, Sarah Griffin, in Acton, west London. For his crimes Duell was hanged at Tyburn on 24 November 1740 and that should have been that. Just one of the 60,000 executed there and not deserving of any special attention.

Except that William hadn't quite finished. When his body was conveyed to Surgeons' Hall for dissection, and he was just about to be cut open, it was found that Duell was still alive.

They bled him and two hours later he was sitting up again, groaning but unable to speak. That night he was back in Newgate prison and the next day he ate well and asked for his mother. Multitudes turned up at Newgate to stare at the resurrected Duell. Somebody behind the scenes took pity on him and rather than make him go through it all again, he was transported abroad.

Here is a little made-up story to illustrate how words and phrases we use these days have made their way over from the realm of crime and punishment into popular usage.

One night a hell-rake (in other words an amoral troublemaker, usually a member of the upper classes) was out with his friends and for fun they turned over a watch box containing a Charley watchman (the phrase 'right Charley', meaning a bit useless, comes from the usually aged and somewhat hapless Charley night watchmen). Unfortunately this particular Charley died.

All the carousers were carted off to the Clink (the prison in Southwark which has become a generic name for all prisons). In the same cell was a man with a skeleton in his closet, (grave-robbers literally had skeletons in their closets). This notorious resurrectionist had turned to murder instead of waiting for people to die.

Also in the cell was a thief and counterfeiter of coins who had been double-crossed, Jonathan Wild the notorious eighteenth-century thief-taker, had an account book in which a thief who paid him received a cross by their name; when that thief was betrayed to the authorities (who also paid him), a second cross went by the name, i.e. they had been double-crossed.

The next day the judge pronounced the death sentence on them all. They were all going to go west (you went west along Oxford Street to Tyburn execution site). En route, the prisoners all had 'one for the road' (a free drink was given to prisoners at a pub along the Oxford Street route). Some of the condemned had arranged for hangers on (the 'hangers on' were the friends and relatives who would, for a price, be allowed to pull on the hanging person's legs so they would die more quickly).

At the site the crowd shouted hats off to those wearing tall hats, so that their view of the dangling human puppets would not be ruined.

TYBURN CONVENT

8 Hyde Park Place, London W2 2LJ. Open daily 10.30a.m.–6.30p.m. Tel: 020 7723 7262. Website: www.tyburnconvent.org.uk. Tube: Marble Arch.

The convent has a model of the gallows and a macabre little collection of details and relics of the 105 Catholics executed at Tyburn.

3) The Process Church of the Final Judgement Mayfair HQ

Balfour Place, London W1K. Tube: Marble Arch.

Travel to Marble Arch underground station. Take exit 2 and walk down Park Lane, skirting Hyde Park which will be on your right. If you like, you could stop to read this section there. After 10–12 minutes, on your left will be a street called Mount Street. Walk into Mount Street and in 1–2 minutes on the right will be Balfour Place. At the bottom of Balfour Place turn left, and there is The Audley pub.

LOVE, PEACE AND SATAN, MAN

Balfour Place is a very short street with some very well-kept and obviously extremely expensive buildings which date from the 1890s. It might be hard to believe, given that the Mayfair area is clearly a very salubrious one and such

42

houses are worth millions of pounds now, but it is true that one of these buildings in Balfour Place was the headquarters of an exceedingly bizarre, not to mention disturbing, late 1960s London cult. The house is on the left-hand side but I am not going to give the exact number in case anyone now living or working at the address objects, or gets spooked.

At that time the door had a symbol on it, the Process logo. This resembled four Ps arranged in a wheel, and was an obvious version of a swastika. In the basement there was a coffee bar called Satan's Cave which had huge red lights. Cult disciples wore black capes with paintings on them of the Goat of Mendes (a somewhat scary occult symbol connected in turn to Baphomet, the supposed idol worshipped by the Knights Templar (see page 105) and glorified by Aleister Crowley (see page 9))

The cult was originally London-based before moving to Mexico and then returning to London even stranger than before.

So what was the cult and what did they believe?

Take some Nietzsche and a sizeable dollop of Aleister Crowley, add a pinch of Scientology, and some crumbs of Christianity. Then add lashings of satanism and serve up as a toxic gumbo in a 1965 London about to embrace peace and love. You might say this strange apocalyptic cult, the Process Church, was the (very) dark underside to the hippie generation. Processeans were on a totally different path. The hippies talked about love; the Process preferred to talk about Love *and* Hate, Jesus Christ *and* Satan (and Jahweh and Lucifer). The Process was obsessed with duality and the notion that humans are trapped in a game and that the game/God will have its way. So be it (as the group was fond of saying).

Leaders Robert De Grimston Moore (who had been an architect) and Mary Ann McClean (who had been a call girl) met through Scientology. (Interestingly, Scientology creator L. Ron Hubbard had been influenced by Aleister Crowley but seemed to want to forget this fact later in life).

Robert Grimstone, also known by the disciples as Christ, perfected his Jesus Christ pose physically while bestowing a torrent of high concept, barely comprehensible, verbiage to the disciples, the contents of which became more sinister as the years went by. It is a massive irony that a religion based on yoking together opposites should end up encouraging its acolytes to adopt any one of four templates. Christ. Jahweh. Lucifer. Satan. Mary De Grimston, for example, identified as Jehovian. Robert was Luciferian.

Disciples were told to emulate any one of these templates, depending on their particular psycho-sexual make-up, but warned not to be 'John Gray'. This hated enemy, John Gray, was not an actual person but stood for the majority of people in society who conformed.

Although 'newbies' were supposed to be celibate, to leave their past behind and give all their money to the cult, at the higher levels cult members indulged in strange 'group gropes' directed by Robert and Mary. Children were often separated from their parents because family ties were distrusted, and were brought up by other group members in something approaching a Kibbutz fashion. Some children were not treated very well in this set-up and have complained that they were physically punished for trivial things. To deliberately further destabilise family ties, some children were told that certain men were their fathers who were not actually their fathers. A former member who has bittersweet feelings about his involvement with the cult admits that many children were left 'royally screwed up'.

There were six grades from acolyte to master and, in further weirdness, German shepherd dogs – the Process dog of choice – were also initiates to the cult.

As with Charles Manson's 'Family', getting celebrities onside was a goal because of the money they had and the kudos they lent. Marianne Faithfull, Mick Jagger's iconic girlfriend, was probably not best advised when she appeared in a death pose in 'Process' issue 3.

Forget Mick Jagger and Keith Richard's cod satanism in 'Sympathy for the Devil' – when the Process went for the satanic template they were the real deal (in America they had had meetings with Antony LaVey of the Church of Satan).

The Process satanic template still makes one's skin creepy crawl (the Manson pun is intended since the Process clearly had a lot of time for Charlie and had interviewed him in prison for the 'Death' issue of the Process magazine).

Here are a couple of quotes from the satanic side of the Process.

> *'Release the Fiend within you! ... And the mother that pleads weakly for her child shall see it slain before her. And the woman that pleads palely for her miserable virtue shall be struck down and raped. And he that fearfully pleads for his life shall be cut to pieces ... And stride with SATAN'S army to the End.'*
> *'Satan on War', Copyright Church of the Final Judgment, 1966*

> *'Or is your place within a ruined church high on a hill, no glass in the tall slotted windows, but perfect for the celebration of the Black Mass? The priest in midnight garb, the congregation, men and women unclothed except for the blood red masks upon their faces, stand silent waiting for the presence of the Lord and Master, Satan. A naked girl, fair haired and in the very prime of youth, lies like a human sacrifice upon the altar, snow white against the black velvet of the altar cloth. Nothing stirs, no sound but the sighing of the wind.'*
> *'The Gods on Sex', Process Church of the Final Judgement*

And there was a lot more of that ilk.

At the cult's peak the Process magazine had a circulation of around 200,000 copies and the church was making a couple of million dollars a year (they had moved to the USA by then), but the rank and file began to look askance at the luxury lifestyle of Mary and Robert. Then the pair split up and she kicked him out of the church into the wilderness and it all went downhill and ended with a whimper, not an apocalypse.

Mary ended her days running an animal centre while Robert may or may not work in communications in New York (so maybe he did go a bit Gray in the end!).

4) Broadwick Street Pump

Tube: Piccadilly.

A very appropriate place to read this chapter would be the John Snow pub on the corner of Broadwick Street and Lexington Street, John Snow being the hero of this chapter (although he never touched alcohol himself).

The best way to get to the John Snow pub is to travel to Piccadilly underground station. Shaftesbury Avenue exit and walk up Shaftesbury Avenue until you come to Great Windmill Street on the left. Walk up Great Windmill Street, which eventually intersects at right angles with Broadwick Street. The John Snow pub is right on the left-hand corner where the two streets meet.

To find the model of the pump turn right into Broadwick Street and walk for a few seconds to where on the left-hand side Broadwick Street intersects with Poland Street; the pump model (it's not the original) is right on that corner, with a silver plaque.

SHERLOCK OF THE SEWERS

Cholera is a disease that we regard as exotic these days; we tend to think of countries like India when we hear the word. However, in mid-nineteenth century London it was a very real threat – in 1849 in England 53,000 people died from the disease.

Cholera symptoms were extremely distressing: weakness, sweating, then involuntary urination and defecation over and over again leaving the victim with a raging thirst but also unable to keep anything down. The victim shrivelled up, the skin became grey and death-like while the face coloration became dark blue and sometimes almost black. Then came coma leading to death that was a relief for many. Two-thirds of those who contracted the disease died from it.

This story concerns the worst outbreak ever in Britain's history. In 1854 a cholera epidemic struck London's Soho district – an area where these days the worst you might feel is a little bit of indigestion after a night out.

Soho had once been a well-to-do area and Broad Street's houses had been sought after in the mid-eighteenth century. One hundred years later, however, it was a poor area and that meant the inevitable overcrowding.

The cholera attack began on 28 August 1854 and in the course of the next two weeks around 700 people died. There were only 49 houses in Broad Street (as today's Broadwick Street was known at the time) and 37 of them experienced cholera deaths. Florence Nightingale was one of the medical staff brought into the area to help the overloaded local medical services.

At the time of this 1854 outbreak 42-year-old John Snow was merely a reserved but effective local doctor who lived just ten minutes away from Broad Street. He had had an interest in cholera for a number of years. At this time it was not known that cholera was waterborne, instead many influential people argued that it was somehow in the air in unhealthy districts (the 'miasma' theory), and could be inhaled, or they thought that it was somehow transmitted person to person like influenza. Those two incorrect ideas were in the ascendency.

After considerable and painstaking study Snow had decided, 5 years before the Soho outbreak, that something in the faeces of infected humans, probably dissolved in drinking water, was the route of transmission. We now know that something to be bacterium Vibrio cholerae although the actual bacillus was not identified until 1884 – 30 years after the outbreak.

Snow's response to the outbreak was a mixture of brilliant detective work and dogged determination – and he effectively did it all on his own. His success was the equivalent of the work of a genius detective successfully stalking a rampant serial killer (which effectively cholera was).

Snow had already noticed that one of the two water companies supplying to south London had moved its base of operations and was supplying water from an area away from sewage pollution. He theorised that if the disease was waterborne then people being supplied water by this Lambeth Company ought to suffer less from cholera than people who lived in the areas supplied by the rival Southwark and Vauxhall Company. He obtained the addresses of people dying from cholera, looked at the postcodes and was able to show that the theory was correct.

When the 1854 outbreak occurred Snow visited all the local water-pumps, including the one on the corner of Broad Street and Cambridge Street, and took samples home but he could find nothing unusual about this particular sample from the Broad Street pump. He decided to try a different method, knocking on hundreds of doors in the district to ascertain if a) anyone in the house was ill and b) which water pump they used. He then plotted the deaths on a map. Putting himself on the front-line in this way was of course very dangerous to his health had the 'influenza' model been correct.

Snow could see that as a result of these independent and logically elegant enquiries, one particular pump, the one outside 40 Broad Street (now 41 Broadwick Street) was implicated. The water from this particular pump had an excellent reputation: it was regarded as the best in the area. Snow, however, managed to convince the authorities to try an experiment and the next day the handle of that specific pump was removed, preventing people from using its water supply. The serial killer was immobilised (although its power to strike had already been diminishing).

Even now Snow's theory was not immediately accepted and it took a further investigation before he was proved to be right. In the meantime the deadly pump was unchained again and used for 12 more years!

The further investigation found that of nearly 300 people questioned who did not use the Broad Street pump, only twenty had been stricken by the disease. The original outbreak was found to be connected to the death of an infant at 40 Broad Street – the house next to the pump –whose diarrhoea had seeped into the drinking water with dire results.

John Snow died at the age of 44 having sold precisely 56 copies of his book on the spread of cholera – but in 2007 workers in the medical profession voted, through the *British Medical Journal*, for sanitation as the most important medical breakthrough of all time.

THREE UNSOLVED LONDON MURDERS

The High Holborn murder

On the morning of Tuesday 15 August 1949, a cleaner ran out screaming from the Adelphi Secretarial Agency in High Holborn, close to Holborn Town Hall. She had just discovered the murdered body of the owner, 36-year-old Daisy Edith Wallis. Ms Wallis had only been renting the back room on the third floor for 3 months. She had been the victim of multiple stabbings by a vicious double-edged knife but the knife itself was missing. Cuts and gashes on her hands and arms showed that she had fought her attacker, but to no avail. Her handbag was still beside her body and it had not been rifled through which meant that robbery was unlikely to have been the motive. In any case, the Agency would not have been a promising target for robbery.

The pathologist identified the time of death at around 6-7p.m. the previous evening. That in itself was very strange because it would have been a time when many people would have been still in the building, or passing it, and therefore a very risky time to commit a murder.

People who had left fingerprints found in the office were systematically eliminated from the enquiry. Only one print could not be traced but whoever left it had never been in trouble with the law because it wasn't on record.

One possible clue was that two people had separately seen a small Italianate looking man, aged about 25–30, running through an alley near the office at approximately the time of the murder, and a chemist nearby had treated a man of similar looks for cuts on his hands.

Miss Wallis proved to be hard to find out about. She had been quiet and efficient and also discreet about her private life. She lived at home with her parents.

She had not stood out while shopping or attending any one of the arts-related clubs she belonged to. Her diary was combed but gave no further clues.

With no weapon or motive, and despite 700 interviews of everyone in the diary or in the office filing cabinet, the police investigation ground to a complete halt and has remained that way ever since.

Marie Bailes: an unsolved child murder

On 30 May 1908 the body of a 6-year-old girl, Marie Ellen Bailes, was discovered in an underground public toilet at St George's Road, Elephant and Castle. Her parents had reported her missing the day before, 29 May. On the 29th she had unaccountably left St John's Roman Catholic school in Islington by herself telling a friend that she was going to go home. She never reached home.

The toilet attendant at St George's Road said he'd been cleaning the steps at about 8.45a.m. on the 30th when a man who appeared 'nervous' came in sight holding a parcel contained in a sack. It was a heavy parcel judging by his struggle to carry it, but he managed to take it down the stairs past the attendant. When the man left, the attendant saw the parcel had been left behind and couldn't resist peeking; to his horror he saw the parcel contained a dead, mutilated young girl.

The 6-year-old girl's body was found wrapped in brown paper and with a clothesline knotted around the neck fastened in a reef knot. In addition, both her throat and her chest had been sliced and her legs and arms had been broken and tied to the sides. Sandy soil was all over her face. Some of the child's clothes were missing and had been used as a gag.

The killer was never found despite the always particularly intensive police work that follows the murder of a child.

One bizarre thing: at the inquest a man stood up and said that there were six different clues that indicated a woman had done it.

Note: If this murder, which defeated 700 detectives at the time, was committed today, the killer would probably be in custody awaiting trial within one week. The police would look for DNA evidence on or in the body plus fingerprints on the parcel and would then check the criminal records. They would also concentrate their efforts on men living within ½ km of the child's house because clearly it was an opportunistic snatching and killing since the child had done something unusual by leaving the school by herself and so could not have been stalked and no pattern could have been followed. The police would also question known sex offenders living locally and they would analyse the sandy soil to try to find useful clues to where the girl had seemingly been buried in a shallow grave before being dug up again. They would also concentrate on men in the area with knowledge of both Lambeth and Islington (Lambeth is a long way from Islington and a public toilet there is a very strange place to dump a dead child's body). They would no doubt also pay attention to the fact the clothesline had been tied in a reef knot and try to find out more about the origins of both the clothesline and the brown paper. They would also do microscopic analysis for fibres.

The torso in the basement of New Scotland Yard

On 2 October 1888 the torso of a woman was discovered in a vault among the foundations for the New Scotland Yard building that was being constructed on the Victoria Embankment at that time. Today the building is well known as the Norman Shaw building and the case is referred to as the 'Whitehall mystery'.

Whoever committed the murder (assuming, as is likely, it was the same person who deposited the torso), had taken both risks and pains to do what he did. It is presumed the torso was left at night-time and although there was no watchman on the site at night-time, it was very dark, and it would have been dangerous to have even attempted to leave anything on-site since there were trenches and holes and the vault would have been pitch black.

The site was surrounded by 7ft high hoardings except for one entrance point which was accessed by a little gate with a latch that was moved by a piece of string. A casual person would be unlikely to stumble upon that obscure entrance to the worksite which indicates that probably either the person had somehow some knowledge of the site already, or had done some surveillance as the workmen had gone about their tasks.

An arm which was later found to belong to this particular body had previously been found floating in the Thames on

11 September at Pimlico, and about two weeks after the torso discovery a leg was also found by a police dog, buried near the construction site. Neither the other arm and leg nor the head was ever found. The uterus had been removed and the doctor thought the actual murder had been committed up to two months earlier. The missing uterus is significant because the uterus had also been removed from the second and fourth Jack the Ripper victims.

There must have been about a thousand easier places to dump a murdered woman's torso than this vault and the fact that it was done nevertheless probably indicates that the murderer was trying to send a strong message of defiance to the police, and perhaps even trying to deliberately taint the brand new police building by murder.

This type of defiance and scorn of the police is reminiscent of Jack the Ripper himself, judging by the notorious letters purporting to come from him (although the jury is out on whether most of those, with the possible exception of what is called the George Lusk letter, were faked). The Jack the Ripper murders were still taking place at this exact time, so could he have been responsible? The answer is yes, but unlikely. Although the uterus was missing and that had also been the case with two of the Ripper victims, there is an overwhelming difference between the murders – Jack the Ripper flaunted his handiwork and did not try to hide the identity of his victims whereas the mysterious Whitehall killer went to extraordinary lengths to hide the identity of the victim and in fact she was never identified.

There is a strong possibility that this 'torso murderer' was a second murderer and a strong possibility that he was a second serial killer because other body parts from other unidentified but murdered women were found in 1887 and 1888 in both the Thames and in the Regents Canal. It is an intriguing possibility that the 'torso murderer' was not only demonstrating scorn for the police and tainting their new building but by his actions he was also effectively competing for attention with Jack the Ripper. 'Look,' he was saying, 'I'm out here too, I started before you, and I'm even more brazen than you'.

However, there is a small possibility that it was Jack the Ripper but he had been forced to change his modus operandi for practical reasons. Whitechapel had prostitutes, thousands of them, in situ but there weren't any around the Norman Shaw police building (they would have been very stupid ones), so he could not kill a prostitute and leave her lying there. Instead perhaps, if it was Jack, he killed a woman elsewhere and then (for practical reasons) brought only the torso to the building.

The case still attracts interest because it may show that Jack the Ripper's murders were indeed predated by another, as yet unknown, serial killer.

3 NORTH LONDON

1) 1987 King's Cross fire

Tube: King's Cross.

At the top of the Piccadilly, Northern and Victoria line escalators at King's Cross, there is an unobtrusive little plaque under a clock on the left-hand side as you go towards the Hammersmith & City Line. The plaque states 'In memory of the 31 people who lost their lives in the King's Cross Underground Fire of 18th November 1987'. King's Cross Station is open until about 12.15a.m., Monday to Sunday.

TICKET HALL INFERNO

'I could hear everybody's little prayer to Jesus.'
Ron Lipsius, King's Cross fire survivor.

The King's Cross fire in 1987 claimed 31 victims including a 7-year-old school-boy, stockbrokers, Colin Townsley (one of the 150 firemen who fought the fire), Alexander Fallon and others.

In 2004, 16 years after his death in the fire, Fallon was finally identified as 'Body 115'. His remains at last had a name to personalise and dignify them. Scottish-born Fallon had been 72 and homeless at the time of his death. Living rough in London after the tragic death of his wife from cancer, on that November night he had presumably been inside King's Cross station for warmth.

The King's Cross station fire began at 7.33p.m. on 18 November 1987, when someone's carelessly-discarded match, or possibly a cigarette butt, ignited extensive dry material that had been collecting for years underneath the partly wooden escalator on the Piccadilly line. Chillingly, investigators after the disaster found 18 scorched areas under one of the *other* escalators, meaning that 18 different fires had begun on other occasions but had not developed …

There had been a no smoking rule on the entire London Underground network for the previous 2 years, but it was frequently ignored, especially by smokers who had just endured a non-smoking journey and who were too impatient to wait until they had completely left the station before lighting up.

The frightening speed with which a smouldering matchstick/cigarette butt developed into a 'tiny' fire initially regarded as not very threatening and a bit

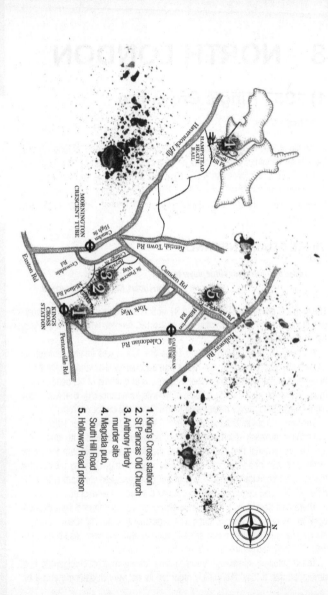

3. NORTH LONDON

1. King's Cross station
2. St Pancras Old Church
3. Anthony Hardy
   murder site
4. Magdala pub,
   South Hill Road
5. Holloway Road prison

'like a campfire', but which then turned in an instant into a raging inferno in the ticket-hall, meant that previously unknown factors were at work. Subsequent research did indeed reveal some new aspects of fire behaviour in certain circumstances, including unusual wind effects in the Underground system caused by trains arriving. The new phenomenon became known as 'the trench effect'.

King's Cross station shamefully lacked routine evacuation procedures or firefighting procedures and when the fire brigade screeched to a halt outside the station and rushed in to tackle the fire they were told staff did not know where the fire hoses could be plugged in. People were being too casual and were severely underestimating what was happening because no one had ever died before from a London Underground escalator fire.

Downstairs, fireman Townsley was just making his way towards a woman whose clothes and hair had been set on fire, shouting to her that she would be ok, when the 'campfire' instantly changed to a colossal fireball of death. Thirty-one people were dead within seconds. Some were burnt to death, some choked to death on fumes and some were poisoned by the cyanide released from the special ceiling tiles.

The massive nature of the fireball was never properly explained but the 'trench' effect and anti-graffiti paint were probable factors.

People who lived through the ordeal described it as 'unreal' or 'surreal'. One minute they were travelling home from work like a thousand times before, in very familiar surroundings; the next second they were fighting to stay alive in the place that they thought they knew so well but was now a hell.

Survivors of such an event often suffer from post-traumatic stress disorder. Shocking images recur to the mind as it tries to process them to be able to move on. Many survivors fell into depression, common among survivors of disasters, because their sense of personal security had been violated so badly. The physical scarring caused by the fire also caused depression.

A feeling of guilt at surviving when friends and loved ones had died was extremely common – the other side of 'why did I nearly die?' is 'why was I chosen to survive?' Then there were the years of painful rehabilitation, the forced abandonment of careers, the toll on relationships and friendships.

> *'My dreams and my aspirations had been put in a bag and thrown out of the window.'*
>
> *Mariella Santello, King's Cross fire survivor.*

At least one person managed to gather strength from the disaster that had befallen her:

> *'Now because I have experienced a greater degree of repression and pain I can
> also experience greater joy.'*
>
> **Rosalind Leech, King's Cross fire survivor**

The King's Cross fire report made 157 recommendations and the management response on the night was attacked as utterly inadequate.

One mystery was never explained – three different doctors who were on the station to see if they could help, all spotted human remains, a thirty-second victim, and yet the pathologist could find no trace of that person.

2) St Pancras Old Church

*St Pancras Old Church, Pancras Road, London, NW1 1UL. Tel: 020 7387 4193
Open: all day from approx 9a.m. until dusk. Tube: King's Cross.*

Leave King's Cross station by the main Euston Road exit. Turn right and walk for about 5 minutes until you come to Midland Road on the right. Walk into that road and then it's about a 10–12 minute walk up that road (which changes to Pancras Road) until you find St Pancras Old Church and its churchyard on the right-hand side. You can go inside if it's open or there are some benches in the churchyard. Incidentally, if you leave the church and turn right, you are only 3–4 minutes away from the location mentioned in the Anthony Hardy story (page 60).

DESECRATING THE DORMITORIES OF
THE DEFUNCT

> *'Night after Night, with crow and spade
> He drove this dead but thriving trade'*
>
> **Thomas Hood, 'Jack Hall'**

On a cold moonless November night in 1810 three black clad men met up for a drink at The Golden Lion pub on the corner of Britannia Street and Grays Inn Road. Later they went for a walk and ended up helping each other over the wall at the conveniently isolated St Pancras Old Church churchyard, not far from modern day Euston station.

The men had with them a large black bag containing a number of items: a dark-coloured sheet; a long rough grey sack; and a small special lantern that curiously and deliberately reflected only a small amount of red-coloured light. Also two small spades and a 'Jemmy', a crowbar which could be used to splinter wood. There was also a length of rope with an adjustable noose at its end. Two of the men were approaching middle-age and occasionally swigged from bottles of spirits. The third man was younger, in his late twenties, and slightly better dressed than the first two. He stood somewhat apart from the others as they approached a patch of earth at the end of a row of gravestones. As the two other men scanned the patch of earth for booby-trap devices (some unpleasant surprises such as triggered gun blasts had awaited 'fishers' in recent years), he scanned the darkness ahead of them where the official church entrance lay, alternately blowing on his hands and gnawing on one of his fingers.

The special lantern's deliberately poor light showed the earth to be a different colour at that specific spot – there had been an interment that very day. But the men knew this already from a contact at the funeral parlour.

One of the men took a long drink from one of the bottles, spat, cursed the cold, and began to dig.

He dug at speed for 15 minutes after which the second man took over for another 15 minutes. At the end of half an hour between them they had excavated a hole about a foot wide and some 6 feet deep. This hole extended to the wood of a coffin, at the head end. The special crowbar was inserted where the coffin lid met the coffin sides and a sharp sustained levering upwards splintered and broke the wooden lid.

The watcher man momentarily glanced towards the hole then resumed his lookout. Next the rope was introduced and within another 60 seconds, and with a careful twist, a dead female adult's body was hauled out of the grave in a perverse parody of a birth.

The preceding scene is a reconstruction, stitched together from many sources, of what a typical body-snatching episode was like in London in the early nineteenth century.

At its height – say in 1810 – the London body-snatcher community might have numbered some 200 men (female body-snatchers were unknown), of which maybe 40 were full-timers. We know about the characters and activities of some of these men from court records, newspaper reports and a hugely important diary by body-snatcher Joseph Naples.

Naples mentions Pancras Old Church a number of times in his diary. For example:

> *'Thursday 2otk. Met and went to Pancress**
> *got 1 5 large & i small took them to Barthol w.'*

(In other words he and a friend went to Pancras Old Church and dug up five adults and one baby and took them to St Bartholomew's Hospital to be sold to the doctors there…)

Body-snatcher men appear to have been somewhat similar in character to Charles Dickens' Bill Sykes. Tough, mercenary, not overly squeamish or slow to violence, often drunks. (Dickens actually has a body-snatcher character, Jeremiah Cruncher, who goes 'fishing' with a spade in this very churchyard in *A Tale of Two Cities*.)

Many would say these grave-robbers were morally indefensible – but how then would you describe the middle-class anatomists and surgeons who bought the bodies and therefore drove the trade?

Medical men at that time had a dilemma. With the explosion of interest in medical science in the late eighteenth century came a large increase in the number of medical establishments, including private ones, and the students who went with them. Suddenly there were about 800 students a year, and students paying high medical school fees expected a real corpse to examine not some kind of model.

Both doctors and students wanted to know all the ins and outs of the human body and the best way to do that was to have a real body to dissect, yet the government was only donating six bodies a year from executed criminals at Tyburn. One corpse per student meant the medical men now needed some 800 corpses a year for the students, not six corpses, so what to do? Also these late eighteenth-century/early nineteenth-century doctors had developed a scientific cast of mind and many had abandoned the commonly held religious fears of the populace surrounding death and dead bodies.

Many ordinary people believed at that time that you could not be resurrected on the day of final judgement if your body was not whole, and it was precisely that fear that was worked on when criminals were threatened with dissection after their deaths.

Some medical men decided there was only one thing for it – bodies would have to be exhumed for the sake of scientific progress (plus financial liquidity of course), and there were certain specialists out there who knew how to do that – for a price. So a strange alliance was forged between the criminal class and the middle and even upper classes.

Many a society mansion in Kensington or Chelsea was visited at odd hours of the night by rough-looking individuals and hurried conferences would take place at back doors. The rough-looking men were never invited inside the mansions but they were nevertheless to be treated with a certain bonhomie after a price was agreed. The money paid out would handsomely reward the specialists for the 'thing' or 'subject' they had brought with them (words like 'body' and 'corpse' were never mentioned on either side).

A student lodging with William Hunter, surgeon brother of John Hunter of Hunterian Collection fame (see page 24), writes to his sister in 1793, 'There is a dead carcase just at this moment rumbling up the stairs and the Resurrection Men swearing most terribly'.

The most famous medical man of the time, Sir Astley Cooper no less, the King's doctor, was heavily involved in this underworld.

In fact, when body-snatchers/grave-robbers/ sack-em-up men (or as they preferred to be known, resurrectionists) went to prison, which they frequently did, the medical men like Cooper would look after their families financially until their release. Cooper would later tell an 1828 Select Committee that 'there is no person, let his situation in life be what it may, who if I was disposed to dissect, I could not obtain. The law only enhances the price, it does not prevent the exhumation'.

The cosy arrangement between the medical profession and the murky world of grave-robbers was brought into the light in 1831 when grave-robbers Bishop and Williams were brought to trial in London. These two and their colleague May had come to the conclusion, like their more famous colleagues in Scotland, Burke and Hare, that waiting for people to die naturally was not a good way of maximising profit. Murdering people would provide more dead bodies instantly and would maximise profit. The economic logic was sound even if the moral stance was queasy.

Ironically, some body-snatchers were probably earning as much as some of the people at society parties, just not in a respectable way. We know from the records (particularly Joseph Naples' diary) that individual corpses were commonly sold for between £3 and £8. Some would even go for £14. In 1810, £14 would represent a comfortable living for 3 months! These especially lucrative 'subjects' would be particularly interesting specimens, e.g. very big or very small or perhaps afflicted by a tumour, or marked out in some other way.

Ben Crouch, the leader of the best-known gang of body-snatchers, told the 1828 Select Committee that he had sold 23 bodies from four nights' work to three anatomy teachers. His share of the proceeds must have been close to £100 that week which would be the equivalent today of over £4,000. Some body-snatchers made as much money in three nights' 'fishing' as the ordinary working man could make in a whole year.

Dead babies, by the way, might be sold for 6 shillings for the first 12 inches and then 9 pence per inch thereafter.

Surprisingly perhaps, the penalties if you were caught body-snatching were not as stiff (pun not intended) as might have been imagined. Body-snatchers caught in the act would often only go to prison for 6 months to 1 year. After all, who owned the actual body? The tenant had departed. Stealing the grave-goods, e.g. jewellery and clothes was more clearly theft, and carried a higher penalty, so savvy snatchers would usually leave the jewellery and clothes behind.

The end of body-snatching can be precisely dated to 1832 when the Anatomy Act was passed allowing the unclaimed dead from workhouses or the street to be given straight to the surgeons. Immediately body-snatching was fatally undercut.

1) *Sometimes grave-robbers pulled out the teeth of the dead with pliers. These were then sold on to make up dentures for rich people.*

2) *Body-snatchers were often rank hypocrites – many left sums of money in their wills to ensure that they themselves were buried extra deep so that they would not be body-snatched!*

3) *In 1997 a rather shocking and disturbing discovery was made: human bones from at least four adults and six children were found under the former house at 36 Craven Street near Trafalgar Square of Benjamin Franklin the American diplomat and scientist. Had he been a serial killer? The answer is more likely to be that these were bones thrown away after anatomy lessons given by William Hewson, anatomist, who had lived in the house. It is extremely likely therefore that some of the bones were from people who had been robbed from their graves.*

4) *Jonathan Wild (see page 40) was grave-robbed from here and his body sold to the Royal College of Surgeons.*

3) Anthony Hardy

Tube: Mornington Crescent.

Travel to Mornington Crescent underground station, exit and walk round the station to the other side where you will find Crowndale Road to the right of Koko Nightclub. Walk down Crowndale Road for some 7–8 minutes to where the road intersects with Royal College Street on the left. The curved modern building on that corner intersection, with lots of brown brick and glass and balconies and a little section on top with a curved white roof, is where the College Arms pub used to be, where two dismembered victims were found in black bags in December 2002. Now turn left into Royal College Street and the first turning on the left is College Place. Walk up College Place using the right-hand side. After about 30 seconds or so you will find the Hartland Block of flats on the right-hand side and a square open space which has a new light brown coloured bench. If you sit on that bench you are approximately 20 seconds from the flat where at least three brutal murders and dismemberments took place (I am not going to identify the precise flat because people live there – although it has been exorcised).

'BONECRUSHER'

Sixty-year-old Anthony Hardy's life is a grim catalogue of alcohol abuse, antisocial behaviour, and failed relationships with women followed by physical or mental attacks (or both) on them, culminating in the murders of three prostitutes. We know for certain of three murders, but it is possible there are more. When the police used ultraviolet light to inspect his room, they discovered the names of three women etched on the wall and then painted over: Sandra, Jayne and Tracy. We have no idea who these women were and what they meant to Hardy or, indeed, if they are further victims.

Six foot tall, hulking and bearded, Hardy was born in 1951 in Burton-upon-Trent in Britain's Midlands. He lived there and married and had four children. The family lived in Australia for a while but his wife divorced him after he mounted a 2 year campaign of intimidation against her which included bugging her house, ringing her multiple times, throwing bricks through her windows and slashing her tyres. This was after an earlier incident which had resulted in Hardy spending time in a psychiatric unit after he admitted trying to kill his wife by first hitting her on the head and then trying to drown her, only stopping when his 8-year-old daughter came into the bathroom and started screaming.

Back in London after serving 2 months in prison for breaking the order forbidding him to harass his wife, Hardy found himself alone and on the slide. His alcohol abuse steadily increased, as did his troubles with the police. At this stage Hardy was drinking seven to eight bottles of cider a day. Social services were notified about him and he began a never-ending round of appointments with numerous well-meaning institutions and individuals connected to Community Mental Health services, all of whom tried their best to help him with his alcohol problems and to stabilise his life. For a time, independent living seemed to be working but Hardy repeatedly missed appointments and more than one person who had dealings with him wrote in their report that they were wary of his strength and unpredictability and afraid of what he might do.

No organisation that had dealings with Hardy seemed to know exactly what his psychiatric diagnosis was and this vagueness undoubtedly helped him stay free. He was, however, described as untrustworthy, manipulative and emotionally detached, classic psychopath qualities.

Meanwhile Hardy's sadistic fantasy world was developing deeper roots and he began to tell people that he had a number of different personae. Worryingly, he sometimes referred to himself as Hannibal Lecter; at other times he said he was an entity 'who hurt prostitutes'...

In December 2002, the police acted after a campaign of intimidation by Hardy against a neighbour in Camden, north London. Hardy had made threats, written abusive comments on her door and put car battery acid through her letterbox.

When the police interviewed him in his room, they found a locked door which they had to force him to open. His reluctance to do so was explained when the police found a dead naked female body in the room with a bucket of hot water and a sponge nearby. There was also a photographer's lamp. The body had a bite mark on the thigh (proven to have been inflicted by Hardy) and various other bruises. Next to the body the woman's tights and bra had been cut into pieces.

Hardy was arrested but his grandiosity (a typical serial killer trait) must have increased considerably when he was released due to the opinion of a consultant pathologist that the woman, 38-year-old Sally Rose White, had died of an unrelated heart attack and that there 'were no marks of violence'! This particular pathologist was later suspended for 4 months as a direct result of the case.

Now Hardy was back on the street again, with only loose monitoring. Another round of appointments with day centres and psychiatrists took place but after yet again emerging from a psychiatric unit, Hardy was about to begin his final descent into perversity and serial killing.

In December 2002 a tramp rummaging through black bags at the back of the College Place Estate (where the modern brown brick and glass block of flats is today) found human limbs. The pieces proved to be the dismembered bodies of 34-year-old Bridgette MacLennan and 29-year-old Elizabeth Valad. Their bodies had been hacksawed and neither head was ever found. Police raided Hardy's flat (which had high-heeled shoes on the window sill). They then revealed that photos of both girls were found in Hardy's room, their faces covered by demonic masks put on them after their deaths. In the light of this, Hardy had probably been about to photograph the first victim when he was arrested. He had once left a Halloween mask in the bed of his ex-wife when she made it clear that she wanted nothing more to do with him.

Hardy said that the two dead women must have suffocated accidentally when he fell asleep on top of them during bondage sex. However, there is evidence that Hardy deliberately crushed each of the women beneath him when they were in their bondage gear before strangling them. He had similarly attempted to crush another sex worker (who had survived), and he had previously been nicknamed 'Bonecrusher' because he enjoyed intimidating people, in hostels for example, by giving them painful extended bear hugs that would leave them gasping for breath.

Hardy was arrested on 3 January 2003. He eventually pleaded guilty at his trial and was sentenced to life. Controversially, he was assessed as having been mentally normal at the time of the killings.

Although he has subsequently found religion in prison, Hardy was told in 2009 that he would never be released – one of a small number of British prisoners to have this 'whole tariff' status. Other serial killers who feature in this book and who have also been told they will die in prison, are Dennis Nilsen (page 7), John Duffy (page 155), Colin Ireland (page 131), and Levi Bellfield (page 159).

4) Magdala pub

2a South Hill Park, London, NW3 2SB. Tel: 0207 435 2503. Open: Monday to Thursday 11.00a.m.–11.00p.m. Friday, Saturday 11.00a.m.–midnight. Sunday 12.00p.m.–10.30p.m. Nearest station: Hampstead Heath.

Travel to Hampstead Heath railway station on the Richmond/Clapham Junction to Stratford overground (not underground) line. Probably the best way to connect with this overground line from the Tube system is at Highbury and Islington underground station on the Victoria line, then it's only five stops to Hampstead Heath rail station.

Leave the station and immediately on your right is a road called South Hill Park. Walk up that leafy road and in less than 3 minutes you will be at the Magdala pub on the left-hand side.

There can really only be one place to have a drink while reading this, The Magdala pub itself. If you don't know why already, have a look at the first paragraph below. If you take a girlfriend or boyfriend here for a drink, make sure you are getting along well. The owner drily describes the pub's style as 'well-executed simplicity'...

I don't know of another London site where the bullet holes arising from a murder that took place over 50 years ago can still be seen at the location all these years after the event. Amazingly, the largest of the three bullet holes can clearly be seen on Google Street View to the right of the first green door before the main entrance door.

HELL HATH NO FURY...

Here, outside the Magdala public house on Easter Sunday 10 April 1955, 28-year-old platinum blonde Ruth Ellis fired five bullets in a 'cold frenzy' (her words) – the last one from a distance of inches only – into her lover, David

Blakely, killing him. She thereby ensured that she would become the last woman to hang in Britain.

Immediately after shooting Blakely, Ellis tried to shoot herself in the head but the gun would not work. Her very first words to the detectives who arrived to question her were 'I am guilty'.

Ruth Ellis and David Blakely were star-crossed lovers, albeit of a different kind to Shakespeare's Romeo and Juliet. Their story reveals the tawdry side of the 50s.

Neither Ellis nor Blakely, her victim, were particularly attractive characters. They were both shallow. He slept with any woman he could, including his close friend's wife. Ellis came from a poor background. The poverty at home she experienced, followed by waitressing and dead-end jobs, made her desperate for money and ambitious for a better social position, and she was not too fussy as to how she achieved it. She became progressively harder and more brittle as her life progressed from nude modelling to occasional prostitution to working in, and then managing, hostess clubs. She learned to use her looks to take men for a ride and could be cold, ruthless and grasping.

She married a rich alcoholic called George Ellis but the marriage quickly collapsed. Her cynicism towards men is revealed by her statement about George, 'I did not get fond of him only to the extent of what he could spend on me'.

Lover Blakely was another bad choice: he was weak and feckless. Blakely's circle was more sophisticated than Ellis's: she had had left school at 14, and there was an element of class warfare in their relationship. Ellis thought that Blakely himself and some of Blakely's friends looked down on her.

Their 3-year relationship was nothing if not volatile. Both of them could be vicious. She threatened him with a knife (he told friends), while he had kicked her in the stomach causing the miscarriage of what would have been her third child with three different men. Both were jealous, Ruth of various floozies in Blakely's life, and Blakely of Ruth's much put-upon 'sugar daddy', Desmond Cussen.

In fact the relationship could have been described as a poisonous, and ultimately murderous, cocktail of lust, jealousy, fear, masochism and brutality. Perhaps there was even room for some love too but both were regularly covered in bruises inflicted by the other.

From the point at which her attempt to shoot herself failed when the gun stuck, Ellis had a death wish and refused all attempts to help her mount a proper defence. It is possible that a case could have been constructed which would have given her a reasonable chance of getting a manslaughter charge, but Ellis baldly told the court that she had intended to kill Blakely when she shot him, and after that statement the judge was always going to be donning the black cap.

Ellis said she wanted to die and wrote to David Blakely's mother that she would still love her son at the moment of her death and that her death would cancel out his.

Many people were uneasy at Ellis's death sentence. Less than ten per cent thought executing her was a good idea. A 50,000 signature petition to commute the sentence was ignored. Even the trial judge Havers had recommended a reprieve in his trial report but the Home Office refused (his grandson, Nigel Havers the actor, found this out).

Albert Pierrepoint, her executioner, was anonymously sent a cheque for £90 (quite a lot of money in those days) not to perform the execution, but makes the point in his autobiography that he felt there was a certain false hysteria around Ellis. After all, he says, he had been due to hang two other women within the same 3-month period and practically nobody said anything or mounted any campaigns for those other executions to be stopped (one was reprieved). He also categorically denies that his leaving the hanging profession had anything to do with Ellis's execution, which he said was nothing out of the ordinary for him and no different from any of the other approximately 20 women he had hanged.

He does however state that women were generally braver than men in their final moments and when on 13 July 1955 Ruth Ellis was hanged at Holloway Prison she did go very bravely, and silently, to her death.

To slightly modify Shakespeare, 'Nothing in her life became her like the leaving of it'.

As she died there were about 1,000 anti-death penalty protesters outside but it made no difference because both the State and Ruth Ellis herself believed in 'a life for a life'.

Only 2 years later, but 2 years too late for Ellis, the law was changed by the Homicide Act 1957 to allow for mitigating circumstances – diminished responsibility – to be taken into account in such cases, and just 10 years after her death the death penalty was provisionally erased.

In 2003, the Court of Appeal was asked by Ellis's sister and daughter to look at the case and consider if the murder conviction could be overturned. They did look but Lord Justice Kay said that as the law stood at the time the conviction was the right one. However he added, 'If her crime were committed today, we think it likely that there would have been an issue of diminished responsibility for the jury to decide'.

What happened to the people she left behind?

Desmond Cussen was extremely lucky not to be charged with being an accessory to murder since Ellis admitted the day before she was hanged that he had supplied her with the gun.

Tragically, both Ruth Ellis's husband, George Ellis, and Andre her son committed suicide. Daughter Georgina wrote a book about both their lives in which she made it clear that she repeated most of her mother's mistakes including prostitution and choosing violent men. She died of cancer at the age of 50.

5) Holloway Road Prison

Tube: Caledonian Road. The location is the same although the old-style prison was completely rebuilt in the 1970s. There are two stone griffins from the old prison in the grounds but they are not visible to the pubic.

Travel to Caledonian Road underground station. Exit onto Caledonian Road. Turn left and walk for 3–4 minutes until on the left you come to Hillmarton Road. Turn left into that road and walk for about 10 minutes until it intersects with Camden Road. Cross the road in front of you to the tall (obviously!) red brick buildings of Holloway Prison.

First you might want to have a drink in the red and white-painted Castle Bar on the right hand side just at the top of Hillmarton Road where it intersects with Camden Road.

EXTINGUISHING INNOCENCE

If ever the dark side of the Victorian era was revealed, it was in the practice of baby-farming. At that time small ads could be found at the back of various newspapers and magazines purporting to come from caring motherly types who wanted to bring up unwanted infants. Some idea of the size of this murderous business can be gleaned from the fact that when a false ad was inserted to check the response, over 300 replies from baby-farmers were received.

Infants were often the products of liaisons between a household servant and the master of a house but at that time illegitimate children were only the responsibility of their mothers – the fathers had no legal requirement to do anything for their children.

Many women therefore had an intolerable decision to make since having a child out of marriage was seen as a terrible disgrace. You could bring up your child by yourself but lose your job (and probably also your housing since the two were often linked), plus face a lifetime of whispers, sneers and pitying looks. Or you could hand over the child to somebody else to bring up, someone like Amelia Sach...

Sach ran a house in East Finchley as a discreet place where unmarried mothers could give birth to their children before their babies were fostered out to others. 'It would be for the best' is what the compromised and vulnerable mothers were told.

Baby-farmers like Sach would commonly offer two options. The first option was a weekly rate, the second was called a premium rate, in other words a one-off payment to look after the baby for good and with no need to stay in contact. A few baby-farmers genuinely looked after the children in their care – but some were psychopaths who took the money and then treated the children appallingly.

Those babies whose parent/guardian had paid the weekly amount were barely fed so that most of them languished and died fairly quickly. An unobservant doctor could usually be found to state on a death certificate that the child had died of 'convulsions'.

Then there were those babies whose parent had chosen to pay the one-off payment. This was a higher amount, typically £25–40, but it can easily be seen that there was a strange discrepancy between even £25–40 and the real cost of looking after a child for, say, 15 or 16 years until he or she was an independent adult. This strange discrepancy seemed to go unexamined by those who felt their lives were burdened by the existence of a child.

The idea of a one-off payment was appealing to some people for the obvious financial reason – the total outgoing expense was less – but sometimes it was appealing for another reason and a deadly understanding was being played out in public. A fee was effectively being paid by people, who could not bear to do it themselves, for others to terminate the life of an unwanted infant and keep it quiet.

In the case of those babies for whom a premium had been paid, the psychopathic baby-farmers would usually just murder their charges and then dump the bodies in such places as hedges and rivers. Baby-farmers would sometimes justify their actions by claiming that they were 'angel makers', doing poor mites a favour by putting them out of a miserable existence.

Many women took up Sach on her offer of looking after their baby for them. Of course Sach would charge at least £15 as a one-off payment for long-term care.

Once the baby was handed over to her, Sach would get in touch with her older accomplice Annie Walters who would dose the babies up with chlorodyne until they died. Chlorodyne was a powerful medicine which included both opium and cannabis and was used to treat insomnia in adults. If they were too long a' dying they could always be smothered.

Walters was unintelligent and her last address was in a house whose landlord was a policeman. The policeman and his wife knew she was a foster parent and the policeman's wife even helped Waters with the nappy of one child but couldn't help noticing that the child disappeared to be replaced very shortly thereafter by a different child, and so on. When Walters asked a lodger in the house to buy chlorodyne for her it was time for the police to be informed and both Walters and Sach were placed under surveillance. When Walters was stopped at South Kensington station in November 1902 she had a dead 3-month-old baby (surnamed Galley) with her. The baby had a noticeably bruised head but Walters claimed she had not known the child was dead until she had been stopped. A police doctor observed however that the dead baby's 'jaws were clenched, toes turned inward, hands tightly clenched'.

The jury took just 40 minutes to sentence the pair to death and here at Holloway Road prison on Tuesday 3 February 1903 an unprecedented event (in modern times) took place: the double hanging of two women, Amelia Sach (age 29) and Annie Walters (age 54).

Henry Pierrepoint and Billington performed the execution, the first at Holloway. Henry recorded in his diary the following remark, 'These two women were baby-farmers of the worst kind and they were both repulsive in type'. His executioner son, Albert, reveals in his own autobiography that it was a distressing scene with 'one of the women in an almost continuous faint having to be propped up by my father on the drop'.

Some of Britain's worst serial killers, in terms of sheer numbers of victims, have been female baby-farmers of the Victorian era. Once a baby-farmer murdered their first child (usually by strangulation but in the case of Walters and Sach by poisoning) there was every chance they would murder a second, third and on and on and on. Even after the 1872 Infant Life Protection Act was introduced to try to bring some regulation into child-minding, six more female baby-farmers were hanged: Jessie King, Amelia Dyer, Ada Chard Williams, the gruesome twosome of this story who were executed at Holloway and, finally, Leslie James.

Amelia Dyer was executed at Newgate on 10 June 1896. She murdered scores of infant children and may have murdered hundreds, the true figure will probably never be known. Even worse, as a result of watching her at work, her daughter and son-in-law then got involved in the same business. It's little wonder that Dyer went mad and talked about seeing visions and hearing little birds talking to her (perhaps triggered by the thought of the dead infants coming back to haunt her).

Sach's East Finchley house, still exists, its past unknown by most people. Three hundred items of baby clothing were found there but it was impossible to tell the exact number of victims. Those 300 items make it very likely that at least 20 babies were killed and that means that the anonymous house in an innocuous London suburb is almost certainly the worst British 'house of horror' ever, eclipsing the British houses of Dennis Nilsen (12 dead in one, three in another), and Gloucester couple Fred and Rosemary West (nine in one house, one in another).

THREE LONDON MEMORIALS TO VICTIMS OF VIOLENCE

11 September 2001 attacks in America

Grosvenor Square

This is where the US Embassy is located in London, and on the opposite side of the square there is now a memorial garden dedicated to the victims of the 2001 terrorist attacks in the USA. Of particular interest here, on three long bronze metal strips on a wall behind the porch of the small classical temple, are recorded the names of all 67 UK citizens who died in the attacks.

On the ground a plaque says, 'Time is too slow for those who wait, too swift for those who fear, too long for those who grieve, too short for those who rejoice, but for those who love, time is not.' That is part of a poem which was read in Westminster Abbey during the 2001 memorial service.

The plaque also says 'This garden was created in memory of all those who lost their lives in the 11 September 2001 terrorist attacks on the United States of America'. Hidden beneath is a piece of the World Trade Centre.

London Tube and Bus attacks 7 July 2005

On this date multiple terrorist attacks on the London Tube system and on a bus killed 52 people and injured nearly 800 others. The major permanent reminder is the Hyde Park memorial.

Hyde Park

Prince Charles opened this 7/7 memorial. Between Lover's Walk and Park Lane it consists of 52 metal poles, each 11.5 feet/3.5 metres tall, standing together but in four groups representing the four bombings that day with the appropriate number of poles in each group reflecting the number of deaths in that particular location. The poles have date/time/and location of the different bombings on that date. In addition there is a plaque on the grass 'In memory of those killed in the London Bombings 7 July 2005' which lists all the victims.

Embankment Gardens

Here is a plaque inscribed 'Under this tree people of all faiths and nationalities, united in grief, laid wreaths in memory of those killed on 7 July 2005, following the attacks on London's public transport system.'

Separately there are also plaques at all five affected sites:

1) King's Cross (in the St Pancras western ticket hall)
2) Russell Square (the Piccadilly line tube train actually exploded midway between King's Cross and Russell Square killing 26 people)
3) Edgware Road where six people died
4) Aldgate where seven people died
5) (Tavistock Square has a plaque on some railings close to where the No. 30 bus explosion took place killing 13 people.

There is also a striking sculpture in St Pancras Churchyard facing Upper Woburn Place and close to Tavistock Square dedicated to the victims of the 7/7 bombings.

De Menezes memorial
Tube: Stockwell.

On the wall outside Stockwell underground station is a colourful mosaic of Jean De Menezes' face surrounded by flowers and doves. The main word is 'Innocent'.

Jean De Menezes was a totally innocent man in the wrong place at the wrong time. On 22 July 2005 he happened to be living in a block of flats that the police suspected had a connection to the abortive attempt to blow up the London Underground system the day before. That failed attempt on 21 July 2005 had itself occurred just two weeks after the Tube system was attacked on 7 July 2005 causing 52 deaths.

De Menezes was followed to Stockwell tube station by a surveillance team and an order was given to stop him entering the Tube system in case he was wired up to explosives. A firearms team was immediately called into action and when he sat down on his tube seat they killed him by firing seven hollow point bullets into his head.

An investigation after his death proved he had no connection to terrorism and no warning had been heard by people in the same carriage as De Menezes. The police apologised for the tragedy. However, some misleading statements had been given by the police to the media and also, for example, to the pathologist who had then written that Menezes 'vaulted over the ticker barriers' (as if he had something to hide). He hadn't and such statements had blackened the reputation of an innocent man. Sympathy for the police position – they genuinely thought at the time that he might be a suicide bomber – was badly undermined by the various misleading statements that were issued in the immediate aftermath of the incident.

4 EAST LONDON

1) Jack the Ripper Part 1: Goulston Street graffiti

108–109 Wentworth Model Dwellings in Goulston Street is now the takeaway section of a café called Happy Days. Tube: Aldgate East.

Travel to Aldgate East underground station. If you are coming from the east, turn right on the platform when you leave the train. If you are coming from the west, turn left on the platform when you leave the train. Follow the sign saying 'Toynbee Hall – Way out'. You want Exit 2. Exit onto Whitechapel High Street, and turn right. In about 1 minute on the right is Goulston Street. Walk up that street for about 5 minutes and just after you pass New Goulston Street on the left you will find Happy Days café on the right hand side. Just where the takeaway counter is, under a red awning beneath some green metal frets, is where the graffiti was left. The café actually has some info about the Ripper and this location on the wall inside, and it would be a decent place to have a snack while reading this story…

YOU GO BACK, JACK, DO IT AGAIN

Here the world's most notorious serial killer once left some graffiti which has been endlessly debated and is still mysterious. The location is one of the few concrete links we have left to Jack the Ripper – because of redevelopment and the World War Two Blitz – and will serve to introduce the case…

Jack the Ripper is the world's most famous serial killer responsible for the most contentious series of unsolved murders, ever.

First of all let's boil the case down to its essentials. Jack the Ripper killed five prostitutes in the autumn of 1888 in the East End of London. That much at least is clear.

Or is it?

In fact each individual component of even that short statement has been fought over by Ripperologists, i.e. would-be Ripper experts.

Did Jack the Ripper really call himself Jack or did a journalist make up the name?

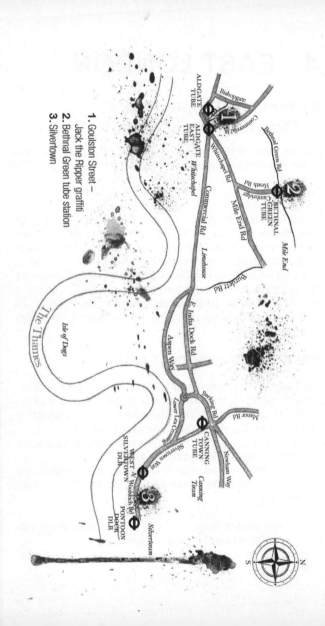

4 EAST LONDON

1. Goulston Street –
   Jack the Ripper graffiti
2. Bethnal Green tube station
3. Silvertown

Did he kill only in the East End of London or did he kill elsewhere in Britain too? Did he perhaps move abroad and keep killing, possibly in America?

Did Jack really only kill in 1888 or were there more victims in later years (and maybe others before August 1888)?

And there are lots more questions …

To be brutally honest we just don't know who Jack the Ripper was. There are a myriad theories but a sensational breakthrough is lacking. That would be something like a genuine diary coming to light (not the one that got published some years back which is regarded by many as a fake), or an authentic series of letters or, best of all (but it's not going to happen), some unprecedentedly long-lived DNA obtained from one or more of the crime scenes matching some unprecedentedly long-lived DNA from a suspect. In their absence we may never know so we are left scrabbling around creating theories based only on circumstantial evidence.

Again being brutally honest, the 'Ripper industry' (which I am a part of) would quite like the Jack the Ripper case to remain inconclusive since certainty is cut and dried and a little bit boring, whereas uncertainty means t here can be endless theories. These in turn lead to a book or two a year, which in turn keep the Ripper industry wheels turning and keep thousands upon thousands of tourists a year visiting the East End of London and paying to come on Ripper tours.

So we don't know who Jack the Ripper was, but we do have theories – boy do we have theories.

Jack wore a leather apron. Jack was a midwife. Jack was a butcher. Jack was a baker. Jack was a candlestick maker (just joking). Jack was a doctor. Jack was a rogue policeman. Jack was an American showman. A German sailor, no, a South American sailor. Jack was Lewis Carroll. Jack was a member of the British Royal family or at least their doctor. Jack was Walter Sickert. Jack never existed. And there are many, many other theories. Probably around 100 in total.

Here is the general background. I am going to deliberately avoid putting the following short account in the past tense because it helps remove the dust of the nearly 125 years that have passed since the crimes. It creates immediacy and helps put you, dear reader, right back at the time almost as if this is a briefing and you are a detective working on this still challenging and mysterious unsolved case.

In the autumn of 1888 in the East End of London someone calling himself Jack the Ripper is killing five prostitutes in 10 weeks. In order of their murders the prostitutes are:

1) Mary Ann Nichols, who is murdered on Friday 31 August 1888
2) Annie Chapman, who is murdered on Saturday 8 September 1888
3) Elizabeth Stride, who is murdered on Sunday 30 September 1888
4) Catherine Eddowes, who also is murdered on Sunday 30 September 1888
5) The last victim, Mary Jane Kelly, who is murdered on Friday 9 November 1888.

They are all either killed or rendered unconscious by strangulation and then have their throats cut. Then in all the cases except one, further mutilations take place while the victim is dead or dying. The mutilations get progressively worse in the course of the murders, with the exception of Elizabeth Stride (because apparently Jack the Ripper is interrupted immediately after her murder and so does not get a chance to mutilate), until Mary Jane Kelly's unprecedented butchery after which the murders seem to stop.

The murders take place late at night or early in the morning. They take place on Fridays, Saturdays or Sundays. The perpetrator takes unbelievable risks and gets away with it since no-one is ever charged with the murders. He seems to court attention and enjoys sending the police, the media and others taunting letters and parcels but some of them may be fakes. Strangely, he appears to disappear completely after the fifth and last murder in November 1888. All the murders occur in the course of just 10 weeks. The fourth murder takes place slightly further away from the East End in the jurisdiction of the City of London police, the rest being in the jurisdiction of the Metropolitan police. He removes the uterus of the second and fourth victims as well as the left kidney of the fourth, and the fifth victim's heart is never found. He evidently works very fast to do the organ removals leading to speculation about his skills. There is no evidence of sexual intercourse.

In fact there is practically no evidence at all but one very important piece of evidence we do know of is the Goulston Street graffiti. After killing third victim Elizabeth Stride and fourth victim Catherine Eddowes in just one hour, Jack the Ripper then passes through Goulston Street where he apparently proceeds to write some words on a wall and deposits a portion of apron that belongs to Catherine Eddowes's apron.

The exact words he writes are hotly disputed because police incompetence at the time means that they are not recorded properly. He either writes 'The Juwes are the men That Will not be Blamed for nothing' or 'The Jewes are the men that will not be blamed for nothing' or 'The Juwes are not The men That Will be Blamed for nothing'. What do these words signify? Do they indicate that Jack the Ripper is himself Jewish. Or is this an attempt to scapegoat others?

The dropped piece of apron means we have concrete evidence (sorely needed in this case) about Jack's movements on the 'night of the double event'. He kills Long Liz (as Elizabeth Stride was known), then heads further west and over the boundary into the quasi-autonomous City district for the first and only time. There, and within the same hour, he kills Catherine Eddowes in Mitre Square before doubling back on himself and heading east since Goulston Street, where the graffiti and apron is found, is 5–10 minutes *east* of Mitre Square. That ruse of crossing police boundaries could be the action of a devilishly clever man who knows that involving two separate police forces is the best way of screwing up police work on a case.

That is exactly what happens – the two forces argue with each other when the Goulston Street graffiti is erased on the orders of Charles Warren, police commissioner who fears reprisals against local Jews if it remains. With that erasure hugely important evidence – Jack the Ripper's actual handwriting – is destroyed. That handwriting could have been compared to the Lusk letter handwriting and to other letters purporting to come from the killer. It would also possibly have afforded the opportunity to detect if Jack the Ripper is left or right-handed.

At this point you may want to visit page 113 where you will find part two of this look at Jack the Ripper and where I identify a suspect after taking into account the facts of the case and the conundrums.

By the way, if you get lost in the Whitechapel area, just ask a passing Ripper tour where Goulston Street is; if you wait 60 seconds a tour group should come along ... !

RIPPER-CONNECTED BURIALS

1) *In Tower Hamlets Cemetery Park, the Llewellyn Family vault contains the remains of Dr Rees Ralph Llewellyn. He was called out to examine Mary Anne Nichols's body on the morning of 1 September 1888. Later that morning Llewellyn performed her post mortem.*

2) *Montague John Druitt's uncle, Robert Druitt, a famous surgeon, is buried in Kensal Green Cemetery in London.*

3) *The five victims of Jack the Ripper.*

   ■ **Mary Ann Nichols** – *City of London Cemetery. Aldersbrook Road, Newham, Greater London, E12 5DQ. Grave 49500, Square 318*

- **Annie Chapman**– *Manor Park Cemetery, Sebert Road, Forest Gate, London E7 0NP. Tel: 020 8534 1486.*
  The grave has now gone. She was buried in a communal grave which has been reused. At the time there was some writing by the grave which said 'Within this Area lie the Mutilated Remains of Annie Chapman, who was interred here in Grave No. 78 on the 14th of September in the year 1888'.
- **Elizabeth Stride** – *East London Cemetery. 230a, Grange Road, Plaistow, Newham, Greater London E13 0HB. Tel: 020 7476 5109.*
  Grave 15509. Square: 37
- **Catherine Eddowes** – *City of London Cemetery. Aldersbrook Road, Newham, Greater London, E12 5DQ.*
  Catherine Eddowes was buried on Monday, 8 October 1888 in an elm coffin in the City of London Cemetery, in an unmarked (public) grave 49336, square 318. Square 318 has been re-used for part of the Memorial Gardens for cremated remains. Eddowes lies beside the Garden Way in front of Memorial Bed 1849.
- **Mary Jane Kelly** – *St Patricks Roman Catholic Cemetery, Langthorne Road, Leytonstone, E11 4HL. Tel: 020 853 92451*
  North-eastern corner.

2) Bethnal Green tube station

Tube: Bethnal Green.

Bethnal Green tube station is on the Central line. When you pass the ticket barrier, turn sharp left into the Roman Road exit. Once you're halfway up the stairs, look behind you, where you will see a small plaque above eye level. Its last words are 'Not Forgotten', but many people have found this tiny plaque inadequate to commemorate what was the worst civilian disaster in World War Two; in fact campaigning pressure means that work is finally about to begin on a much bigger memorial to the dead to stand outside the station – more details at www.stairwaytoheavenmemorial.org.

'NOISE AS YOU'VE NEVER HEARD IT'

On 3 March 1943 at 8.27p.m. precisely a tragedy began to unfold at these steps leading down into Bethnal Green tube station. At the time, during the

Blitz, underground stations were being used as air raid shelters and this was the biggest one in the entire area. It could hold up to 10,000 people but at the time of the incident only a few hundred people had been coming regularly to the station.

On this particular date, several separate factors conspired to produce a disaster. Firstly, Londoners were aware that German cities were now being heavily bombed and there was a nervousness about retaliation on London. This meant that when the air raid warning went a larger than normal group of people began to run for the steps. Many were women with children.

Secondly, there was a salvo of rockets from nearby Victoria Park at 8.27p.m. just before the woman slipped. The exceptionally loud noise panicked people and even more people ran, leading to a crowd developing around the entrance to the station wanting to get inside as soon as possible. Panic is infectious.

A woman holding a child in the leading group at the bottom of the stairs stumbled and fell. Somehow another man fell to her left. With the building pressure of the crowd shoving forwards, the people immediately behind those that had fallen in turn had no choice but to fall, and so on. The people crowding in at the entrance began to feel that something was wrong but they wrongly concluded that they were being refused entrance and so pushed even harder. Within 15 minutes 173 people were dead: 27 men, 84 women and 62 children. The toll would have been even worse had a number of babies not been passed overhead to safety.

At the bottom of the steps was a wall of fallen human bodies, five or more deep. The cause of death was suffocation. Although attempts were made by wardens and others to extricate people, the horribly tangled mass of bodies was practically impenetrable. It took hours to accomplish and by then all hope had long, long gone.

The official report (kept secret for years) declared that ultimately the only thing that would definitely have helped would have been the permanent presence of a policeman or woman to keep good order among those descending the steps. With overstretched police in a war situation it was clearly impossible to have such a guaranteed presence. That meant nobody really was to blame and there the sad story ended.

Until a rumour began.

What had actually caused that noise at 8.27p.m., seemingly from the direction of Victoria Park? The government was silent on the question but some people started to dig around for information and a disturbing theory emerged.

It turned out that Victoria Park had just taken a consignment of Z-Battery guns. This was a new weapon of real ferocity designed to destroy enemy planes. It could fire 64 twin rocket projectors producing shell bursts covering a square mile of sky, but it was still experimental and only fired 14 times during World War Two. The downside of that ferocious power was a ferocious noise.

No-one associated with the Victoria Park Z-Battery has ever talked, although the Ministry of Defence has now confirmed there was one there, but soldiers who worked with the Battery elsewhere have talked about it. One said 'The sound made by the salvo was completely awe-inspiring in its noise and ferocity'. Another said 'It was as if all hell had been let loose, belching out flame and noise as you've never heard it'. A third soldier said 'Everyone else who heard it would be the same as me – petrified'.

Could this terrifying sound, heard for the first time in the area, have triggered the panic that led to the deaths? The official position is that the panic was caused by other factors but who wants to admit to accidentally killing your own? There may well be more to come out on this subject in the future.

3) Silvertown explosion

Nearest station: Pontoon Dock on the Docklands Light Railway. It takes about 30 minutes on DLR (Docklands Light Railway) from Tower Gateway station to Pontoon Dock. Tower Gateway is itself about a two minute walk from Tower Hill station on the Circle and District lines. When you are on the DLR, change at Canning Town for the Woolwich Arsenal Line. Pontoon Dock is on that line.

After leaving Pontoon Dock, as you look at the road, turn left. To make sure you are walking in the right direction, you will pass under a small metal bridge after a few seconds. Walk along North Woolwich Road for 5–7 minutes and you will find the monument to the victims on the left at the entrance to Minoco Wharf.

The monument is a small, white, freestanding stone about the size of a man, and can easily be missed, so keep your eyes peeled. It also doubles as a World War Two memorial and in fact you have to walk around it to see the side that talks about the factory victims of this explosion. A metal stand a few feet away gives extensive information about the disaster. After looking at the stone and reading the information I suggest you cross the road. The pavement on the other side goes up a little hill, which is high enough to let you look back over and see the large area where the explosion took place – it was never rebuilt. I then suggest you follow that pavement down to the right (i.e. the direction you were originally walking in) and within a few minutes you will come to the red doors of LFCDA – London Fire Brigade Silvertown Fire Station. Here you will find a little plaque to the firemen killed in the explosion.

The area is unsettling, desolate and has an almost surreal atmosphere. I recommend it as an experience in itself – there's nothing like it anywhere else in London. I would not necessarily come here late at night!

TOTALLY NEEDLESS TRAGEDY

There are explosions – and then there are cataclysms. At 6.52p.m. on Friday 19 January 1917 a cataclysm hit east London when 50 tonnes of high explosives blew up at the Brunner Mond Works south of the Royal Victoria Dock in the East End.

It was the biggest explosion in London's history and all of London heard it and felt it. People 100 miles away heard it. The area was ripped apart and torn up. Sixty thousand houses were damaged (there was housing for workers just 200 metres from the explosion). Lumps of metal showered down over a wide area starting further fires. A gas holder went up in a massive fireball. A fireman later wrote about the places that caught the full force of the explosion, 'it was as though a giant pestle had descended from the heavens and pounded them to powder'.

Andreas Angel, the handsome chief chemist at the Works was killed fighting the fire. He received the Edward medal posthumously. The local fire station, on North Woolwich Road and right next to the works, was demolished and local firemen paid a very high price in the disaster. Firemen Henry Vickers and Frederick Sell went straightaway to the Brunner Mond Works to fight the fires. They and the other firefighters in attendance must have felt a sense of doom (like the firefighters who went to the Twin Towers site in New York on 11 September 2001) because they all knew that there was a terrible risk of explosion, given the nature of the plant. They were killed. Other firemen were very seriously injured and one fireman lost his wife and three children. Also police Constable George Greenoff was shepherding people away from the area of the factory when he was hit by debris and killed.

The official death toll was 73 people (there are now thought to have been some more deaths that went unreported at the time and about a dozen bodies were never identified). One hundred more people were badly injured and hundreds more incurred minor injuries. Many others suffered severe shock and some people became 'unhinged'. This was out of a local population of 4–5,000. In the following days, the Prime Minister, King and Queen all visited the scene.

Although the deaths and injuries clearly constitute a tragedy, the truth is that a much, much worse situation was only narrowly avoided and the death toll could have been ten times higher had the explosion taken place just a couple of hours earlier when there were far more workers around.

Originally a factory that specialised in making soda products, in World War One a fateful decision was made to convert the Brunner factory into a TNT (high explosives) purification works. The government knew it was dangerous but just crossed their fingers and gambled. The chief scientist of the Brunner works said later, '… every month we used to write to Silvertown to say that their plant would go up sooner or later, and we were told it was worth the risk to get the TNT. One day it did go up…'.

Given the dangers (even if there hadn't been a war), it is incredible that the factory was allowed to be situated where it was. Oil refineries and gasholders plus other chemical plants were all close by. With the glaringly obvious dangers multiplied in the case of war, the factory was simply a disaster waiting to happen. A month before the disaster did happen a government inspector had paid a visit and in his follow-up report he wrote, casually but ominously,

> *'It is perfectly clear that the management at Silvertown did not pay sufficient attention to the explosion risk attached to the handling of the TNT.'*

Yet it was not a war incident that triggered the disaster since London was free from air raids that day.

Could it have been sabotage? Perhaps it was fire that caused the explosion? The official report came up with no definitive answer but admitted that sabotage 'could not be disregarded'.

The official enquiry was definite about one thing – there should have been no TNT plant at that location. The government suppressed the report for over 30 years …

In the end the government paid out the equivalent of £40 million (in today's money) for compensation claims, but 73 people were dead and a large area devestated, and no compensation could cover that terrible fact.

THREE BLOODY CEMETERIES IN LONDON (AND ONE CREEPY ONE)

Brockley & Ladywell Cemetery

Brockley Road SE4. Tube: Crofton Park.

Crofton Park station is 5 minutes away.

The monument to Jane Clouson is in the Brockley part of the cemetery, slightly apart from other graves. It consists of a vertical pillar with a statue of a beseeching child on top. The inscription runs,

> 'A motherless girl who was murdered in Kidbrooke Lane Eltham age 17 in 1871'.

This was a famous murder case at the time and thousands attended Jane's funeral. Highly unusually, all the pallbearers were women.

Jane was born on 28 April 1854. Her mother died when she was 13 and two of her three siblings also died. In 1871 when she was 16, her employer, by the name of Pook, dismissed her as a parlourmaid because she was 'lazy and unpleasant'. Those assertions were untrue and the real reason for the sacking was that Jane had been having a relationship with the employer's son, Edmund Walter Pook. Clouson was actually pregnant by Pook Junior. Edmund Pook was a strange young man, three years older than Jane, who was in the habit of carrying a whistle and blowing it in the direction of attractive women passing him, as if they were dogs.

On 25 April 1871, the day she suffered a brutal hammer attack, Jane arranged to meet Edmund at Blackheath having told him by letter that she was pregnant. Later that day Jane was found badly battered, with one eye hanging from its socket, barely alive. A whistle lay nearby. Her last words were 'Oh let me die' before lapsing into unconsciousness, but it took five further days before she finally expired.

Edmund Pook was identified by a shopkeeper as the individual who had purchased a hammer from him which was found in a bloody condition a mile from the body. Also, a man matching his description was seen running away from the scene; Pook said he was merely running home. The clothes he wore that day had blood on them. Pook was found guilty at Coroner's court but the case then went to the Old Bailey where, despite the mass of evidence (a total of seven witnesses placed Pook in Jane's company that day but all those depositions were ignored), Edmund Pook was acquitted of the crime. Many felt that the judge had identified with the defendant on a class basis and a strong sense of outrage forced the Pooks out of their Greenwich house. A committee was formed which raised money for this statue.

Camberwell New Cemetery

Brechley Gardens, SE23.

Crofton Park and Honor Oak Park (5 mins) are the nearest train stations.

Plot: 15336.55 – the large grave has a black and gold headstone with a picture of a boxer.

Freddie Mills – former world light heavyweight boxing champion 1948–1950. In 1965 Mills died by a bullet fired through his eye into his brain. He may have committed suicide, or he may have been killed: arguments continue. It is very rare, however, for someone to shoot themselves through the eye when that eye is open, as apparently was the case with Mills.

Mills appeared in two of the long-running series of Carry On comedy films, Carry on Regardless and Carry on Constable but more importantly for this book, he is a persistent, but unproven, suspect in the unsolved Jack the Stripper murders – a series of eight prostitute murders that took place in west London in the 1950s and 1960s.

Chingford Mount Cemetery
Old Church Road E4.

Reginald Kray and Ronald Kray. Section B8

Violet Kray and Charles Kray. Section B8. Grave No. 70707

Frances Kray. Wife of Reggie Kray.

Frances had first attempted suicide 3 months after marrying Reggie. She did commit suicide at the age of 23 just over 2 years after marrying him. Frances's mother detested Reggie for what had happened to her daughter and when he insisted Frances be buried in her wedding dress her mother ensured that her dead daughter was wearing tights and a slip so that her body would not touch the dress ...

And which is London's creepiest cemetery?

My vote goes to **Abney Park, Stoke Newington**. It has a palpable atmosphere, even in daylight, and I would have to be paid an extremely large sum of money to actually spend the night here by myself – particularly since on a visit years ago with my girlfriend, I recognised signs of satanist activity near a ruined building in the cemetery.

5 EAST CENTRAL LONDON

1) The Gladiators Arena

Guildhall Yard, EC2. Admission to the Roman Amphitheatre is free (there may be a charge for certain special exhibitions). Opening hours: Monday to Saturday 10a.m.–5p.m. (last admission 4.30p.m.), Sunday 12p.m.–4p.m. (last admission 3.45p.m.). Tel: 020 7332 3700 for a daily recorded message giving notice of any closures. Tube: St Paul's.

Turn right into Cheapside then after about 6-7 minutes turn left into King Street and after walking about another 5 minutes, at the top of that street on the other side of the road you will see the church of St Lawrence Jewry. The open space called Guildhall Yard is behind the church of St Lawrence Jewry and you need to turn to the right inside the Yard to get to the Guildhall Art Gallery which is also the entrance to the amphitheatre.

MAN'S INHUMANITY TO MAN MAKES COUNTLESS THOUSANDS CHEER

Despite having been Roman London's biggest building, the London amphitheatre had been missing for 100 years until it was finally discovered here in 1988. After a further 15 years of painstaking excavations the public were finally admitted for the first time in 2002.

In truth, when you go underground (because Roman London is some 18 feet or 6 metres below our modern London) there is not a huge amount to be seen but when what you can see is pieced together with what we know about gladiators from elsewhere the whole picture becomes fascinating – and certainly bloody.

The London amphitheatre was built around AD 70 and was made of wood, but it was given a big refit in the second century and bolstered up with more stone and tile. The word arena comes from *harena* the Latin word for sand, used for its ability to soak up lots of blood, and the excavations here found the remains of the drainage system built under the amphitheatre to drain off human and animal blood into tanks.

The amphitheatre was built close to the Roman Fort which itself was located roughly where the Barbican outer is today (a Barbican in Roman times was a

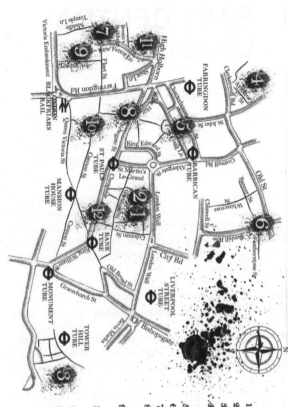

1. Gladiators Arena
2. St Lawrence Jewry church
3. Tower of London
4. St James' Church, Clerkenwell
5. Smithfield – execution site
6. Braithwaite House
7. Temple Church
8. The Old Bailey/ Newgate Prison
9. Kings Bench Walk, Inner Temple
10. St Andrew-by-the- Wardrobe
11. John Wilkes statue
12. Mithraic Temple: Temple Court, Queen Victoria Street

watchtower manned by soldiers overlooking the Roman wall). The proximity of fort to amphitheatre – just a 10 minute walk – strongly suggests that a large proportion of the London audience would have been off-duty soldiers seeking bloody entertainment.

The size of the London amphitheatre was about the size of a modern day football pitch. Compared to the size of the Colosseum in Rome, which held close to 55,000 people, there would have been space for some 5-6,000 spectators at the London one – but the entire population of London at the time would only have been about 25–30,000 people. The Guildhall Yard indicates the dimensions of the arena by means of a curved black line on its surface.

Most of the shows put on here would probably have involved animals and criminals being put to death for public entertainment. The London amphitheatre ruins include a stone with two grooves indicating a wooden trapdoor to let out wild and ravenous animals. However, Christians were probably not thrown to the lions in London because it would have been too expensive to import lions – but possibly they were thrown to wolves.

A day at the amphitheatre would have been in three parts. In the morning wild beasts were killed (a bear skull was found in York's amphitheatre), around midday criminals and prisoners of war were slaughtered, and then later in the day came the main event – gladiatorial combat, the real highlight of their visit for most people.

Although professional gladiators would certainly have fought each other, and animals, here, the men v men shows would have taken place perhaps only 12–15 times a year. That was because those shows were the most expensive since professional gladiators required a lot of training. Those being trained lived in a *ludus* (training school) and there must have been a strange and powerful 'camaraderie of the doomed' in such a place.

The atmosphere at the amphitheatre was a bit like that at a modern football match. There were even memorabilia stalls where you could buy gladiator memorabilia just as people buy football shirts these days.

Our mental picture of gladiatorial combat, built up by such popular films as *Spartacus* and *Gladiator* is not accurate in many ways (let's face it, Hollywood films rarely are). The costume worn by Russell Crowe in *Gladiator* is apparently wrong for a start says the Museum of London. The iconic thumbs up by an emperor to let a gladiator live, or thumbs down for him or her to die probably did not happen; it is now thought that a sideways waggle of the thumb meant death while connecting the thumb and the forefinger to make a circle meant life. Nor did gladiators say *Morituri te salutant* (meaning 'those who are about to die salute you') except on one famous occasion when a sea battle was recreated on an Italian lake. The commentator Suetonius wrote about that occasion and the words took on a life of their own.

By the time the London amphitheatre got going the Romans had already had some 400 years' experience of gladiatorial fighting and had already worked out the most interesting combinations. Some gladiators were lightly-clad which had the disadvantage of offering very little protection to a sword but offered mobility. The retiarius would be that type of gladiator and would use a trident and a net. The heavily armed individuals on the other hand were really weighed down and so slower.

In the same way that in our time, half a crowd at a football match might be there to cheer on, let's say, Arsenal, and the other (misguided) half might be there to cheer on Manchester United, similarly in the amphitheatre half might be there to cheer on the 'Big Shield' man and the other half would support the 'Little Shield' man. These were two styles of fighting. A Big Shield man would have little armour (hence the need for a bigger shield) and would be more defensive whereas a Little Shield man would probably be a more aggressive fighter but with the disadvantage of a smaller shield to ward off attacks.

Not every fight ended in a death but certainly, over time, most gladiators did die on the arena sand. The average life-span of a gladiator was about 28 years and any individual gladiator, even one of the strongest and fittest, would be fortunate to survive five gladiatorial contests. If you did survive five contests you might be awarded the *rudis*, a wooden training sword, and that meant you had won your freedom, would be pardoned if you were a criminal, and could retire with honour. Some who retired went on to become trainers themselves at the *ludus*. Certain macho individuals would sometimes keep fighting. There is evidence of a French gladiator who won 53 fights.

Losers were carted off as so much offal, but first there were special personnel who walked round the amphitheatre. One was dressed as Hermes (Mercury) and would prod bodies with red hot pokers to make sure they were dead and not faking death. If you were still alive you had your skull smashed in by another grim individual dressed as Charon (the ferryman of the dead) to make an end of you.

Contests were usually man v man, There were some female gladiators too, although probably not many and they probably fought without helmets so their beauty could be better observed. Female gladiators sometimes fought male dwarves but new thrills for the audience were always being sought to ward off the 'when you've seen one female gladiator fight a dwarf you've seen them all' syndrome.

The burial site of a London female gladiator was found in Southwark in 2000. She had been burned on a pyre and buried with her was a lamp decorated with scenes of gladiatorial combat.

Even though they might be criminals, individual gladiators (the Beckhams and Messis of their time) had their own followings. A gladiator possessed an ambivalent social status somewhat akin to that possessed by an Elizabethan actor. They were beyond the pale but the successful ones also had a kind of glamour attached to them. After all these were macho individuals in peak physical fitness who lived together and trained hard (using blunt knives). We know from graffiti that some had female fans. From Pompeii we have this – 'Celadus makes the girls swoon'.

Arena entertainment went into decline in the fourth century and the amphitheatre was abandoned by the time the Romans left London in the fifth century. That may have had something to do with the impact of Christianity but there could have been other factors too. Certainly, by the fifth century, after the Romans had gone, there would have been nothing to see here any more, just a grassy space.

2) St Lawrence Jewry church

Tube: St Paul's.

Go to St Paul's underground station (Central line). Emerge into Cheapside and walk along for around 6–7 minutes until you come to King Street on the left. Walk up King Street and at the top you will see the 1680 church by Christopher Wren called St Lawrence Jewry. There is a lily-strewn pond here with a few seats where you can read this chapter.

Look up at the top of the church at the spire with its golden weather vane. There are two secrets here. The first is that the spire is not lead but fibreglass since the original leaded spire was destroyed in the Blitz. On the left of the weather vane is a grille (because St Lawrence was grilled to death by the Romans), but look at the piece of metal on the right. That is the second secret – highly unusually, the metal is a representation of an incendiary device, and therefore it is a memory of Sunday 29 December 1940 and the second Great Fire of London which destroyed the interior of this church and most of the area.

RAINING FIRE

PART ONE: CONFLAGRATIONS

The Blitz on London by the Germans in World War Two started on 7 September 1940 and continued for 57 consecutive nights. It was a war of attrition and parallel to the attempt to destroy London's buildings was the attempt to destroy the morale of Londoners. It was a good ploy by the authorities to accentuate the positive and declare 'London Can Take It' in posters around town, but they knew that 'taking it' would be easier said than done in the face of unrelenting pulverisation and psychological damage.

Then there seemed to be a lull although on Sunday 22 December 1940 a massive incendiary device attack took place on Manchester, ominously foreshadowing what was to happen in London exactly one week later.

Sunday 29 December 1940 was the last Sunday of the year and the City district, which was only lightly populated anyway, and particularly on Sundays, was almost deserted. On the plus side this meant that thousands of people who might otherwise have been killed or injured in the attack weren't in the area; on the negative side it meant that those who were left were going to be more helpless in the face of strikes.

The Germans knew that most businesses in the City did not employ separate fire-watchers but relied on the fire brigade, putting even more pressure on the five fire stations in the area. There were five because successive governments knew that the City was a 'fire zone' where fires could spread quickly through narrow allies and link up with other fires. Firemen referred to City warehouses as 'torches looking for a light'.

The Germans knew that on Sunday 29 December the skies en-route to London and over London were going to be overcast creating tricky bombing conditions. That was a disadvantage; but there was going to be a freakish counter-balancing advantage to going ahead with the bombing raids – the tides were due to be exceptionally low in London that night. That meant that the Thames – London's natural fire-fighting reservoir of water – would have a minimal water level and that would present a crucial advantage to attackers intent on creating fiery mayhem.

The plan was to drop an unprecedented number of incendiaries on the City. Incendiaries were not brute force devices which used many pounds of explosives: they were small and devious 2 pound 'firestarter' devices. One German bomber could carry nearly 300 such incendiaries. A sortie with 20 planes could drop close to 6,000 incendiaries. The Germans were intent on starting the 'second great fire of London'.

At about 6p.m. London time the incendiary rain began, dropped by the German elite 'fire-raiser' squadron. Fifteen minutes later fires were already out of control in the City. The area around St Paul's, which had again become an area of book storage as it had been in Shakespeare's day, again went up in smoke as it had during the 1666 first Great Fire. St Paul's itself was being threatened and an American correspondent erroneously filed a report that it was 'burning to the ground'.

There were now hundreds of incidents – at one point a call was coming through to report a fire every 13 seconds. The fire crews were under the cosh already. Then the City's main water supply was rendered useless by a bomb.

At 7p.m. the roof of St Lawrence Jewry began to burn but there was no-one available to help. The planes attacking from above now had a fiery red glow to help them target the City. At 7.45p.m. Churchill demanded that St Paul's be saved no matter what. He knew that if St Paul's was gutted then the morale of Londoners would be irreparably damaged and people would truly start to believe that London, and therefore Britain, could be conquered.

The air was heating up – rubber soles were melting. Hot air was forced upwards sucking in cooler air in a howling wind that then spread sparks and embers to other buildings. Heat radiated across streets firing the buildings on the other side. A firestorm was being created.

PART TWO: INFERNO FIRESTORM

There was now a brilliant light from the City district radiating across London. So intense was this light that a newspaper could be read by it. St Lawrence Jewry was now collapsing into itself and by 9p.m. there was nothing anyone could do. Somebody wrote in her diary of the 'terrible beauty' around St. Paul's. There were now literally thousands of fires joining together. 'Only' 100 people had been killed by this stage but the fabric of the City was being utterly consumed. Buildings were collapsing everywhere. At about 11.30p.m. the incendiary rain stopped. It started to rain a little and the water from the Thames began to have some effect. By 7.30a.m. the fires were contained and running out of fuel.

When morning dawned it revealed a scene of almost total devastation. The City area on the morning of 30 December looked like a blackened charred skeleton of what it had once been. It had been murdered. A total of some 24,000 incendiaries had been dropped – 300 incendiaries a minute at one point. Two thousand fire-pumps had been in action and 9,000 fire workers had fought the fire. Sixteen firemen were dead and 250 had been seriously injured. Ten Wren churches, of priceless filigree beauty, had been destroyed. Hundreds of little alleys and winding streets had been obliterated and that is why the area there now has modern concrete steel and glass buildings everywhere on a grid system with practically nothing left of the old London apart from the rebuilt Wren churches.

Yet against all odds, St Paul's, the symbol of London and the biggest target of all, had somehow survived.

A photo that went around the world and became an instant classic was taken the night of the 29 December. It shows St Paul's as an embattled icon wreathed with smoke and flames but exuding calm defiance. That is an anthropomorphism of a stone structure but when you look at the photo it's hard not to see it in that way.

The motto of St Paul's is resurgam, 'I will rise', the word on a piece of stone that had been brought to Wren by a worker when Wren asked for a keystone for his Cathedral.

That night the nearly 250-year-old masterwork had endured and the City around St Paul's would rise again.

3) Tower of London

London EC3N 4AB. Tel: 0844 482 7777. Open Tuesday–Saturday 9a.m.–4.30p.m.; Sunday–Monday 10a.m.–4.30p.m.; last admission 4p.m. Tube: Tower Hill.

Travel to Tower Hill underground station (District or Circle lines). Walk outside and look to the right where you will see the Tower itself opposite. The main entrance is a five minute walk from the station through the subway and to the right but you could just stay here surveying the scene and reading this story without actually paying to enter.

SCAPEGOATS

The Tower is a hugely popular tourist destination in London with close to a thousand years of sometimes bloody history. There are very many episodes that could be talked about – the Princes in the Tower, the torture of prisoners such as Guy Fawkes, the raid on the crown jewels, etc etc but here is a lesser-known episode …

The Jews in London in medieval times had their ghetto where 'Old Jewry' is today, near Bank Station. In Edward the Confessor's time (1042–1066) they were under the personal protection (or one could say at the whim) of the King. At the time of the Norman conquest William the Conqueror (1066–1087) brought more Jewish people over with him. Initially all was well but in King Stephen's reign

(1135–1154) fines began to be levied on the Jewish community and security and comfort disappeared. Being direct subjects of whichever King was in power had advantages on occasion but it also meant Jews were not given any guarantees under Magna Carta.

Jews had few options other than being money-lenders, which the Catholic Church at the time forbade. This ability to lend and make money was the very reason why Kings were interested in the Jews and occasionally courted and protected them – but Jews were also disliked by some people for that very same reason (added, of course, to the fact that they were 'different').

Jewish money-lenders charged high interest because they had no security since a King could and would take their money by heavily taxing them whenever he felt like it – and he did not have to seek anyone's permission to do so.

Fom the King's point of view it was taxation of the people by proxy with the great advantage that the Jews were the scapegoats and not him, and when necessary the Jews could always be punished to appease the people. The Constable of the Tower of London was in charge of the day-to-day regulation of Jewish affairs.

Other Kings followed Stephen's lead and recognised that the Jews could be threatened whenever cash was needed. In Richard I's time (1189–1199) there were two outbreaks of violence against the Jewish community, including a massacre the day of the coronation itself, but King John (1199–1216) took vindictiveness to another level by arresting and imprisoning thousands of Jews, blinding some, when they could not pay his swingeing levies.

In 1218 after a decree by Pope Innocent III in 1215, English Jews were forced to wear identifying yellow badges. This was a horrible prefiguring of what was to happen in Germany some 700 years later when the Nazis revisited the idea, even using the same colour.

Henry III's reign (1216–1272) illustrates the ambivalence of Kings towards the Jews very well. When he was crowned, the entire Jewish community in London was shepherded into the Tower to protect them, so there could be no repeat of the riots against the Jews that had taken place when Richard I was crowned. However, Henry then went on to impose a tax equivalent to one-third of the value of Jewish property.

In 1241, in the aftermath of a massacre of Jews in Norwich for supposedly interfering with a Christian child, Henry cynically chose that moment to threaten a well-known London Jew, Aaron, son of Abraham, and others, to pay him 20,000 marks at two payments a year or be confined in Newgate until death. Later still in Henry's reign Jews from all over England were imprisoned in that same Tower because they could not pay his one-third tax and hundreds of Jews were killed in a massacre in 1264 and their synagogue was destroyed.

Massacres like that one often started with a disagreement between one Jew and one Christian but would then quickly spill over into large-scale violence by a Christian mob against the Jews.

Resentments and hatreds were fuelled by false rumours that Jews were secretly ritually killing Christian children and using their blood. This type of rumour is a classic projection of fears and frustrations onto a small and little-understood minority.

The London Jews began to become very familiar with the Tower of London: they were always either being imprisoned or protected there depending on whether they were more or less in favour. So close was the association that there was a Jewry, an official place where Jews were allowed to live, within the Tower boundaries.

Edward I (1272-1307) nicknamed 'Longshanks' made it law that all Jews from the age of 7 years should wear the large yellow badge, and that women should wear it too, but the real hammer blow to the Jewish community in his time was that the Jews were accused of trying to make illegal profits by large-scale coin 'clipping'. 'Clipping' meant either physically removing some of a coin before passing it on, thereby making a profit, or 'sweating' (shaking coins in a bag and collecting the dust).

This was a very serious charge and in 1278, 600 Jews were imprisoned on one day in very cramped conditions in the sub-crypt of the White Tower. Of the 600 some 280 men and women were actually hanged.

In 1290 all 16,000 Jewish people were expelled from Britain and were forced to leave behind their houses and most of their possessions. They were treated terribly during the deportation and many died.

Ironically, after their deportation Kings had to obtain money from the Italian merchants of Lombardy under pretty much the same conditions as the Jews had lent money.

Jews did not return to England until 1656 during Oliver Cromwell's Protectorate.

4) St James Church, Clerkenwell

Tube: Farringdon.

Turn left and left again up Turnmill Street. After about 5 minutes, cross the busy Clerkenwell Road and then take the next right, Clerkenwell Green. Turn left into Clerkenwell Close and the church is in front of you. The opening hours are approximately 10–4 Monday–Friday, but to avoid disappointment check the website: www.jc-church.org. Enter the church and walk ahead for a few seconds. Look at the 'Fenian' plaque on the right at the main entrance to the church nave. It actually understates the full casualty figures. Please note that as well as the 'Fenian' plaque the church also has a 'Smithfield martyrs' plaque to the right of the alter (see page 99).

COLLATERAL DAMAGE

The 'Fenian outrage' plaque here in the church is connected to 'the Irish problem'. From the mid-1860s onwards the Irish 'problem' came home to London with a series of attacks by 'Fenians', supporters of Ireland's independence from Britain, including by armed means. The word was used proudly on one side and as a term of abuse on the other. A series of skirmishes, and sometimes 'outrages', took place from mid-century onwards which seriously stretched the security services in London. Special Branch was set up to combat Irish terrorism.

Among the Irish community in England and in London there were many Fenians and Fenian sympathisers. Militants had adopted a 'cell' system which made it harder to infiltrate them and therefore harder to arrest everyone who might be plotting. A cell leader, called a 'centre', might have nine brothers under him and each of those brothers might have nine further men under him.

The seeds of what was called the 'Clerkenwell outrage' were planted when Richard Burke, one of a large number of American sympathisers for 'the cause', was demobbed after the American civil war and went to Britain to buy arms and ammunition to use against the British. In Manchester he planned a rescue mission for Fenian prisoners who were being transported in a police van. This resulted in two top Fenian prisoners being freed, but also in the death of an unarmed prison guard. Three of the attacking gang were later publicly executed in November 1867.

Along with his colleague Casey, Richard Burke escaped the hunt for the attackers but was arrested on 20 November 1867. On 23 November both men were incarcerated in the Clerkenwell House of Detention, an old remand prison for nearly 300 prisoners situated just outside the old London City wall.

The surface site of the House of Detention was later developed into the Hugh Myddleton school, now private flats named Kingsway Place. The subterranean network of cells and tunnels still exists under the car park there. It used to be a commercial spooky attraction but was closed down in 2000 for health and safety reasons.

Back in 1867 the prison presented a formidable appearance, having an 8 metre/25 foot high wall next to the exercise area. On the other side of that wall was Corporation Row, home to many poor working-class families.

During exercise Burke was observed by prison personnel to pass signals to someone in one of the Corporation Row houses. He had already smuggled out a letter in invisible ink demanding that an attempt be made to liberate them and that the section of wall near a local pub called the Bell was the weak point and should be blown up. He also suggested the best time of day to mount the attack would be 3.30p.m. or 4p.m. Some idea of Richard Burke's character can be gleaned from the last line in the clandestine letter, 'If you do not do this, you ought to be shot'.

On 12 December 1867 some Fenians brought a cart to the prison; sitting on top of the cart was a huge petroleum cask full of 200 pounds of gunpowder. They put the cask beside the wall and fumblingly lit the fuse – but it went out. As nonchalantly as they could the men went off again with the barrel, unchallenged. Amazingly, the next day, Friday 13th (it really is unlucky–see also page 109), at exactly the same time they tried again despite the presence of numerous people, mainly from the poorer working classes, going about their business within metres of the barrel, including a few young boys playing right beside it.

A Fenian tried to light the fuse, but again it refused to light and the man threw it down. One of the little boys actually took up the dud fuse to play with! The man tried again – Michael Barrett was later reported by a plotter turned informant to have been the individual who at last lit the fuse successfully.

In fact the police knew of the plot and had exercised the prisoners in the morning rather than as normal in the afternoon so that there were no possibility of any escapes. Scarcely believably, the police just let the Fenians explode the bomb anyway without alerting the locals to take any precautions.

The bomb exploded at about 3.40p.m. The explosion was devastating: one of the worst in London's history. The row of houses opposite the prison collapsed with the massive rebounding blast wave.

Including those who later died in hospital, nearly 40 people were killed by the bomb and well over 130 were badly injured. Most tragic of all some 20 of the 40 dead were unborn children in their mothers' wombs who were later born dead. Most of the dead were women and girl children because the men were at work.

Karl Marx, who was living in London at the time, said he didn't see why the English working classes should be expected to die for Ireland.

At the trial of the gang, Michael Barrett, stood out from the other defendants as a charismatic, likeable and good-looking individual who was hard to dislike. He gave one of the most memorable speeches ever heard in the Old Bailey.

Many people were crying by its end and some women fainted. In his moving speech Barrett passionately protested his innocence and claimed he had nothing to do with the others in the dock. It was an amazing performance – but it was acting and totally futile since numerous people independently identified him as one of the gang and also one of the female defendants, overcome with emotion, in what can only be described as a 'D'oh' moment, fervently kissed his hand in the court!

Many people felt uneasy when, puzzlingly, only Barrett was condemned to death. The rest of the defendants were acquitted.

On 26 May 1868, outside Newgate Prison, Michael Barrett became the last man to die in public in England. He went into eternity bravely. His death was not enough for some though: Queen Victoria wrote after the trial in 1868 that she was upset about 'the failure of the evidence against all but one of the Clerkenwell criminals ... it seems dreadful for these people to escape ... one begins to wish these Fenians would be lynch-lawed on the spot'.

Indeed after Michael Barrett's execution a derogatory term for the Irish gained currency – the Micks!

In 1973 Michael Barrett's political 'children' in the modern IRA tried to blow up the Old Bailey court building itself by detonating a car bomb outside, leaving a scene of destruction in the street outside akin to the effects of a major hurricane. Unbelievably no deaths occurred but there were many injuries and property damage was extensive.

5) Smithfield martyrs – executed by Queen Mary

Tube: Barbican.

Leave Barbican station (on the Metropolitan, Circle and Hammersmith & City lines), and turn right; in a few seconds turn right again into the street called Long Lane. In about 5 minutes the road opens out into a large open space called West Smithfield. In the centre is a pleasant little garden with grass and benches where you can sit and read this chapter.

KILLING IN THE NAME OF ...

West Smithfield has plentiful associations with the theme of 'horror' or 'bloody' London. This Smithfield (derived from 'smooth field') district lay just outside the

EAST CENTRAL LONDON

BLOODY LONDON

old London wall built by the Romans and because of its outsider status, slouching sullenly beyond the wall, it attracted three major, and frankly unsavoury, activities and trades. These were ones that good citizens didn't want to think too much about – animal slaughter, prostitution, and executions.

Smithfield was synonymous with executions from early on. In the murky depths of London's history there are references to criminals being hanged from a row of elms that grew here (the Elm was regarded by the Normans as a tree of justice), or drowned in a nearby pond. This was around the same time that executions began to take place at Tyburn at Marble Arch.

Spare a thought for Richard Roose, a chef who was boiled alive here in 1531 in Henry VIII's time for a deadly (and quite possibly accidental) food poisoning episode. Roose was placed inside a huge cauldron, the water was heated up and they boiled him to death. It took too long though so by the time they did the same to Margaret Davy for a similar poisoning 11 years later, they put the victim into already boiling water.

In 1305 English King Edward I (Longshanks) had his Scottish bête noir Sir William Wallace (also known as Braveheart) hung, drawn and quartered here, Wallace's head was the first to adorn London Bridge.

Later in the fourteenth century Black Death victims were buried here.

The modern Smithfield square is fringed with bars and cafés. City workers grab snacks and sit in this little garden with the statue with the upraised hand. Most of the buildings surrounding this little park are nothing special but three are very special indeed. The Smithfield meat market (from 1868); the stunning and ancient St Bartholomew the Great (second oldest church in London, dating from 1123) and St Bartholomew's hospital (founded that same year).

St Bartholomew's hospital has a very proud 800 year history record of saving lives. Willam Harvey worked at the hospital 1609–1643 and it was here that he discovered the circulation of the blood.

However, during Queen Mary's reign just 60 years before, in the mid-sixteenth century, every inch of Smithfield had been drenched on a regular basis in that precious blood that Harvey and other surgeons would work so hard to conserve. In 1849 workmen in front of St Bartholomew the Great. found gruesome reminders of those barbaric times: quantities of scorched human bones and a neck collar.

For hundreds of years Smithfield and environs had been renowned for its quarters of animal flesh, its pools of cow, sheep or pig blood, and its slippery animal entrails. In the mid-sixteenth century, however, the haunches were human, the smell from the fires of Smithfield came from burning human flesh, the gushing blood was from men and women, and so were the slippery entrails.

In Tudor times both Catholic and Protestant regimes vied at different times to see who could be the most cruel. Mary's abattoir was at Smithfield, Elizabeth's was at Tyburn and elsewhere. Both acted despite a severe injunction from their joint Christian God (an injunction, too, which apparently had no smallprint), 'Thou shalt not kill'.

Perhaps the worst you can say about the zealots at that time is that their butcheries eventually led, by reaction, to groups like the Hellfire Club (page 122) who abandoned all religion.

Smithfield in those years saw scenes of astonishing bravery and also scenes of fiend-like cruelty.

John Rogers, Queen Mary's first victim, was seen to wash his hands in the fire, apparently serene as a self-immolating Buddhist monk in a sea of flames. The bravery is not in question but Rogers himself had previously sanctioned the burning of Catholic 'heretics'.

Those about to ascend the 'chariot of fire', as the chroniclers of this period term the 'martyrdoms', were bound to a wooden stake with an iron chain. Wood and reeds were then piled up at the bottom to provide fuel for the fire. Some victims were provided with a bag of gunpowder around the neck. When the flames took hold, the gunpowder blew the victim's head off. That was mercy.

Bishop Nicholas Ridley, who had had others burnt and cared not a jot, now leapt up and down under the faggots of wood and screamed over and over 'Let the fire come to me: I cannot burn'.

William Shakespeare (who was no fan of burnings), observed the aftershocks of this bloodiest of periods, and writes about revenge in *Macbeth* with his usual perceptiveness:

> *'… we but teach*
>
> *Bloody instructions which, being taught, return To plague th'inventor'.*

Multitudes of animal corpses are still delivered to Smithfield meat market these days for wholesalers to purchase but only ghosts remain from the years when the sweet and deadly smell from Smithfield assaulted your nose and made you gag.

Now, thankfully, in this little garden in the centre of Smithfield you are looked on by a statue of peace.

St James Church, Clerkenwell gives the names of some of the Maryan martyrs, i.e. victims of Queen Mary. In the interests of balance you might want to go to Ely chapel, Ely Place (15 minutes away) and see a stained glass window of Catholic 'martyrs' being put to death with a creepy Henry VIII watching their agonies in the background, plus statues to the memory of the 105 Catholic 'martyrs'.

6) Braithwaite House

Tube: Old Street.

Travel to Old Street tube station and leave the station using the Old Street exit. Walk down Old Street and in about 5 minutes you come to Bunhill Row on the left. Walk down Bunhill Row and in about 5–6 minutes you will see a large tower block on the right-hand side just before Chequer Street. That is Braithwaite House.

CARVING UP LONDON

On 8 May 1968 at 6a.m. a criminal empire collapsed here at this tower block when the police raided Violet Kray's flat on the ninth floor and arrested her sons, the twins Ronnie and Reggie Kray. When the police piled in they found Reggie in bed with a girl and Ronnie in bed with an underage boy. In the end there was no shoot-out, no explosions. They went quietly, Ronnie Kray simply repeatedly asked that he be allowed his psychiatric stabilising medication. They were never to be free men again.

The Krays were identical twin gangster brothers who came to prominence in the 1960s. Ron and Reg were born and bred in the East End of London and bound together by a closeness that bordered on telepathy. Apart from the shared genetic makeup, they also shared a bond of violence that the saner brother (Reg) just could not bring himself to break. When Ron, a homosexual paranoid schizophrenic, (Reg was basically homosexual too but, unlike Ron, not happy about it), brutally murdered a gangland enemy in an East End pub in broad daylight, Reg knew he would have to kill someone too or lose the respect of his brother.

You could make a film …

Kray supporters (and not all are ageing East Londoners) often come out with one or more of the following sentiments:

'They were only looking after their own community'.

'At least you could walk the streets in those days and leave the back door to your house unlocked'.

'They only killed other villains'.

'They did a lot for charity'.

The British 'Monty Python' comedy team brilliantly satirise the Krays in their 1970 'Piranha Brothers' sketch. The Brothers apparently had been born 'on probation'. One of them takes an interest in 'boys' clubs, sailors' homes, choristers' associations, scouting jamborees and the grenadier guards'. He goes into a nightclub with a friend 'carrying a tactical nuclear missile. They said I'd bought one of their fruit machines and would I pay for it'.

It's extremely funny stuff, but only because by the time it was written the Krays were behind bars forever.

The reality at the time had not been quite so funny so let's wipe the vaseline from the lens and look clearly at what actually went on. The Krays grew up tough from an early age. In the East End mean streets they were meaner than the rest and as young tearaways they were marked out by a combination of ferocity and fearlessness. Later this lack of fear plus the unpredictability of their outbreaks of violence would bring them the craved-for respect.

Their first Old Bailey appearance was aged 17 but the case collapsed when witnesses were too terrified to appear. That same year the police assessed Ronnie Kray as follows, 'Ronald Kray ... will not hesitate to kill in any circumstance'. This would prove to be accurate and prescient. Indeed it is amazing that it took as long as it did for murder to be added to the charge-sheet.

The twins started off small and local, in the East End they knew inside out. A bit of fraud here, a bit of 'protection' there. From there it escalated to bigger frauds, building an ever bigger 'firm' or gang, and penetrating ever further into the lucrative West End world of gaming clubs and nightclubs.

The brothers cared about image. Famous sixties photographers took pictures of them. They had carefully studied the Mafia and were trying to do a similar thing in London. Cockneys Nostra, if you like. Capone and the rest of Murder Inc wore dark glasses and sharp suits, so the Kray brothers dressed that way too. The Mafia used exploding dumdum bullets for executions so Ronnie Kray modified bullets to achieve the same horrendous effect (although he didn't get a chance to use them). Ron's favourite actor was Mafia-connected George Raft; the twins arranged to meet him in London.

What they were actually doing, despite the naive assertions by some about their community-minded spirit, was attempting to build a criminal empire based on fear, as the Mafia had done. The charity donations were just to look good and keep the locals onside. The Krays only cared about themselves (and their mum, of course).

In the booming late 1960s in an ever-widening radius from the East End, pubs and clubs that were making money were visited by the Krays who demanded a cut for 'protection'. If you refused to acquiesce to the repeated demands for 'protection' money (essentially so you could be 'protected' from the Krays!) you paid for it in blood. You were battered or cutlassed (razors were 'babyish' said Ronnie, 'you can't put no power behind a razor').

If cases ever went to court, jury members would be nobbled (threatened) to ensure that either the cases collapsed or the 'right' verdict was given.

As time went on in the newly egalitarian decade, the Krays succeeded in making pals in the sporting and showbiz industries – even in parliament – through certain shall we say, 'partially sighted' unscrupulous Lords, actors and sportsmen. Some people got an almighty thrill out of consorting with thugs and murderers, utterly ignoring the plight of shopkeepers and others who quaked at the mention of them.

If you were loyal to the brothers you could make lots of money but if you argued with them and showed a lack of respect you might end up dead – as the cases of George Cornell, Jack 'The Hat' McVitie and Frank Mitchell demonstrated, and those are just the ones we know of for definite. Cornell and McVitie in particular were deeply unpleasant people. They were 'heels' – both had a record of beating up women – but neither deserved to die the way they did.

Cornell made the fatal mistake of brazenly venturing into the East End the night after a shoot-out in south London left a Kray associate dead. He was already in Ronnie's little black murder book for calling him a 'fat poof' to his face. It's never a good idea to taunt a psychopath about his weight and sexual inclinations, especially not one with a penchant for the old ultra violence and an ache to become a killer. When Cornell and a few pals looked up from their drinks in The Blind Beggar pub to see an undisguised Ronnie Kray and accomplice striding into the pub, Cornell casually said 'Well look who's here'. A few seconds later a bullet had penetrated his brain. He'd been shot between the eyes. Later Ronnie would admit that killing George Cornell had sexually excited him – never a good sign.

Jack 'The Hat' McVitie's death was even more gruesome. McVitie had stolen some Kray money, which was his death warrant. Invited to a party in Stoke Newington, north London, he was set upon by a bunch of men. He almost escaped from a window but was dragged back into the room where Ronnie held him from behind while brother Reggie stabbed Jack multiple times, finally pinning him to the floor through the throat. The body was never found.

Now the twins were equal again. Reggie had 'done his one' too and wouldn't have to put up with Ronnie's taunts that he'd gone soft.

Huge in body but small in mind, Frank Mitchell regarded the Kray twins as 'the two best friends a man could hope for' and never more so than when they sprang him from prison. Mitchell would have died for the twins and when he became a volatile liability, he did. Although neither pulled the trigger on that occasion they arranged for the shooting and after Mitchell was given 'four injections in the nut' (bullets in the brain) he was still alive so he was shot more times in the heart too. When the coded message came through after the murder that 'that dog is dead', Reggie had a little cry while Ronnie wanted to hear more details of the shooting.

It was policeman Nipper Read who took the Kray empire down. He organised mass arrests of the gang and then cleverly worked on the weaker members to give evidence against Reg and Ron. One trait the twins clearly failed to import successfully from the Mafia was their code of omerta or silence – 28 criminals gave evidence for the prosecution at the trial of the Krays and the twins copped 30 year minimum sentences.

Ronnie's funeral in 1995 was the biggest since Winston Churchill's and brother, twin and lifelong partner-in-crime Reggie was let out for the occasion (although discreetly handcuffed to a tall policeman). He was mobbed by well-wishers and supporters. Reggie himself died 5 years later.

Ronnie had named his pet snake Nipper after the detective who pursued them relentlessly, but Nipper Read had the last laugh when he put the twins away for life. It seems appropriate to let him have the last word with the unvarnished truth about the Kray twins,

'… they were wicked, unscrupulous, murdering villains'.

7) Temple Church: Knights Templar headquarters in Britain

Opening times vary. Check website for details: www.templechurch.com or ring 020 7353 3470 to check current opening times. Entry charge: £3. Free to children, senior citizens, members or staff of the Inns or of Chambers and those who would like to come to say a prayer (you will be directed to the east end of the church). Tube: Blackfriars.

Travel to Blackfriars underground station. Exit and cross the road in front of you. Turn right and walk up New Bridge Street and in less than a minute you will find Tudor Street on the left. Walk into Tudor Street and continue to the end of that street where you will find a little archway which should be open during daylight hours (it shuts at midnight). Walk through the archway. Turn right and walk up the hill between the cars until you see the 'Library' sign on the left. Go through another archway there and you will see the Temple Church immediately on the right. Try to avoid the uneasy feeling that among the sharp-suited lawyers who work in this area you caught a glimpse of an albino monk...

After your visit you can exit to Fleet Street via Inner Temple Lane, just past the Temple church on the right.

POWERPLAY

'For where God hath a temple, The devil will have a chapel.'
Robert Burton, Anatomy of Melancholy, 1621

Quite a number of people set out to find this ancient Temple Church dating back to 1185, but some don't succeed because it is hard to find; a hidden location that belonged to an enigmatic and secretive organisation, or as some would say, a cult.

However (to the disappointment of some no doubt), this chapter does not propose to treat *The Da Vinci Code* as anything other than a novel, or delve into even more elaborate theories which end up as books with titles like 'The Templars, the Pyramids and Bigfoot' (only joking, but you know the genre I mean).

You don't need to get quite so far-fetched to find the story of the Knights Templar, whose church this was, a remarkable, tragic and still mysterious one.

It is a story of a dizzying ascent to power, wealth and privilege, followed by a precipitous descent to immolation when on Friday 13 October 1307 luck dramatically deserted the Knights Templar and they were arrested en masse on the orders of French King Phillip IV ('Phillip the Fair'). This King Phillip has been accused of cynically seeking the Templars' riches under the guise of rooting out heresy. The pope at the time was Clement V and he appeared to be unable to resist the move by Phillip and to cave in afterwards.

Eventually the word went out that Templars were to be arrested everywhere, including in England, but before the story of the fall from grace, logically the story of the ascent should first be given.

The Knights Templar Order was founded by Hugh de Payens in 1118/1119 to protect and guide the thousands of pilgrims who visited Jerusalem. After Saladin captured Jerusalem in 1187 a more military vision came into focus, which was to battle the Saracens and to try by means of a series of crusades to reclaim Jerusalem from 'infidel' hands. The Templars (and their rivals the Knights Hospitaller) became the military wing of Christianity.

From the beginning the Templars had a certain ambivalence about them: they were soldiers but they were also a religious order, easily identifiable by their white cloth robes with the red cross. The Templars proved to be doughty fighters and won some battles against Saracen military leaders, becoming hero-worshipped for their bravery and chastity. However, as time went on they also became the bankers of rulers throughout Europe and beyond. They amassed huge amounts of property (19,000 manors), became incredibly rich, and dressed well.

The problem was that the original rules of the order had clearly stipulated that they were to remain humble. For example, they were supposed to wash the feet of poor and sick local people and invite them for dinner. As time went by, this happened less and less and cronyism developed whereby more attractive and politically useful allies were invited to share in the spoils of conquest while poor people got trivial alms if they got anything at all. Other people could wash the feet of lepers.

Now back to the situation in France (this is necessary before dealing with what happened in England). The accusations against the French Templars, and therefore by default all the Templars, were stunning and for many observers simply unbelievable. They were accused of having abandoned Christianity and having turned to devil worship. There were also accusations that Templars had actually covertly converted to Islam after long years of battling the Saracens in the Middle East.

The torturers began their work to find out the truth, as they would on 'witches' in the not too distant future, and with a similar result. The problem with torture is that when it is used on people they will generally tell you whatever you want to hear because, quite simply and understandably, they want the pain to stop. Most will confess even if they never actually did what they are accused of.

So after the wave of arrests and once the tortures began, Templar after Templar confessed that when he had joined the order there had been a secret reception ceremony in which he been ordered to spit on Christ on the cross, had watched members giving each other obscene kisses around the anus, been told that sodomy was good, and been told to worship a strange idol's head called Baphomet.

Could it be true? There is no doubt that the Templars had fallen massively into the sins of pride and arrogance but the big question – the Baphomet in the room so to speak – was had they really turned to devil-worship? Or were they rather the innocent victims of political and religious in-fighting and intrigue? Or could the truth lie, as so often, somewhere in between?

One very important factor here was that under torture, the Grand Master, Jacques De Molay, who was in his mid-sixties, admitted he had done such things and was publicly paraded saying it. Once *he* had confessed there was always going to be a wave of confessions because it's hard to keep going under torture when your leader doesn't.

But when the Templars were out of the torture chambers and able to make their plight known to the wider world, suddenly they rallied. De Molay retracted his confession and scores of others did too. The imprisoned Templars appointed some feisty leaders with legal expertise to take on their accusers and they were making good headway when those leaders simply disappeared. Clearly they had been murdered behind the scenes. This hammer blow to the Templar hopes was followed up by the *coup de grâce*. A new commission took over the investigation, with the powers to immediately execute people, and that is what happened. The due legal process was halted and in 1314 burnings began. Philip the Fair had won.

Faced with flames De Molay found courage and again recanted his confession to heresy and devil-worship and declared the Order was innocent of the charges against it.

Now to the situation in England, then under the rule of Edward II (1307–1327). At first Edward did nothing because he didn't believe the charges, but then he came under pressure from the Pope and the word went out to arrest the Knights Templar.

In 1309 and 1310 some of the English Templars were interrogated in the church of All Hallows by the Tower, an ancient church still there today by the Tower of London. It was perhaps no coincidence that because England did not allow the unrestrained tortures that had been used on the French Templars, there were far fewer confessions. It probably helped too that the English Grand Master, unlike De Molay in France, held firm under the permitted tortures, but some of the oldest members could not withstand them and confessed to denying Christ. They promised to come back to Christ and were forgiven. No Templar was executed in England.

Fourteen years later Edward II seemed to be having trouble sleeping at nights because in 1323 he gave away all the Templar lands and properties, which had reverted to him when the Order was broken up, to the Templars' fierce rivals, the Knights of St John Hospitaller.

Were the Templars heretics and devil-worshippers? Probably not. Some members may have done some strange things over the years, this was an arrogant secretive society after all, but it is too huge a coincidence (in other words no coincidence) that the heretical sect, the Cathars, had previously been accused of practically the same things: renouncing Christ, the obscene kiss, etc.

What was the strange head that the Templars were meant to have secretly worshipped? The descriptions by individual Templars under torture are incredibly vague and contradictory. Some said it was brass, some said it was wood, some said it was called Bahomet, some said Mahommed (fitting in with the charge that some Templars had gone over to the other side), some said it was of a woman, some said it was bearded, etc. In other words people acted as if they were being forced to describe something under torture that they had never actually seen.

In 2001 a document was found in the Vatican secret archives which showed that Pope Clement V had pardoned the Knights Templar in 1307, seven years before the fires consumed them, but crucially, he did not make the pardon public because he feared a church schism.

SOME LITTLE-KNOWN FACTS ABOUT THE KNIGHTS TEMPLAR

1) Norwegian fanatic Anders Breivik killed 77 people in July 2011 in twin attacks on Oslo (eight people dead) and the island of Utoya (69 dead). He spent his first year in London and lived at the Norwegian Embassy at 25 Belgrave Square, London SW1X where his dad was a diplomat.

Breivik claimed to have attended a meeting In London in April 2002 to reconstitute the Knights Templar.

2) It is believed by some that, rather than referring to the day and attendance figures of Christ's Last Supper, the mass arrest of the Templars on Friday 13th October 1307 is the real reason Friday 13th has been regarded as a day of ill omen ever since

3) One of the newer drugs cartels in Mexico calls itself the Knights Templar. They actually have white robes with red crosses and their own Templar rule-book. They claim to be fighting poverty and injustice as they mass traffic drugs, and demand secrecy from members or their families will be killed.

8) The Old Bailey and Newgate: court and prison

The Old Bailey, London EC4M 7CH. Tel: 020 7248 3277. Opening times: Monday to Friday, 10a.m.– 1p.m. and 2p.m.– 5p.m. Website: www.oldbaileyonline. org. Tube: Barbican.

Travel to Barbican tube station. Leave the station and turn right; in a few seconds turn right again into Long Lane. Walk down that street until it opens out into West Smithfield and then turn left. When you see the ancient church of St Bartholomew the Great on your left turn right and walk down that side of the square for about 5 minutes until you intersect with a street called Holborn Viaduct. Cross over and just to your left will be the huge bulk of the Old Bailey Central Criminal Court. The entrance is in the newer building further on down. The Old Bailey has been erected on the site where Newgate prison stood.

NOTORIOUS NEWGATE

Until 1902 when the prison was demolished, Newgate was located where the older part of the massive Old Bailey court complex is today; some of Newgate's stones were used in constructing the Old Bailey.

Newgate had an evil reputation from the very beginning. There were no TVs in rooms here … The first definite references to the Newgate Gatehouse prison (the prison was originally actually within the structure of the City Gate at Newgate) are from the thirteenth century but it was probably in existence 150 years before that time, not long after the Tower of London was constructed. The medieval prison was simply described as 'terrible'.

To be committed to Newgate to wait for a trial could well be a death sentence, even if you had done nothing wrong. The constant overcrowding led to frequent outbreaks of gaol fever (often typhus) which would periodically rage unchecked in the prison, killing both prisoners and guards and, on occasion, judges and even Lord Mayors.

In 1750, 100 prisoners were awaiting trial in two tiny rooms. Some of the prisoners, the Lord Mayor, two judges and some members of the jury died – a total of 40 people. There was no in-house prison doctor in those days.

Many of the guards were extortionists who could make an already unpleasant life far worse, plus innocent people awaiting trial were forced to live in dank dungeons, without light or change of air, and with all kinds of criminals including some of the most violent and debauched. The food was scant and of poor quality since the worst food in the city, which ordinary citizens refused to eat, would be given to the prisoners. Bread boiled in water to make 'soup' was a common meal.

Cells were damp, with pools and rivulets of human sewage on bare stone floors, and all the poorest prisoners had to sleep on were filthy rags or bits of besmeared straw. Unlike modern prisons, there was no hour a day in an outside yard for exercise, indeed there was no exercise at all. Instead, prisoners lay there all day and night with intolerably heavy leg-irons (legally meant only to be used on prisoners who had attempted to escape but instead used indiscriminately on all). Some prisoners could have their irons taken off if they could pay for it, and in fact all kinds of improvements were possible, including decent accommodation, if you could pay. Such payments to ease one's way in prison were known as 'garnish'. Obviously if you were in Newgate for debt (which half at least of the prisoners were) then you had no chance of paying for any of these improvements, and many a murderer was treated better than a debtor.

The condemned hold was particularly terrible with nothing to sit or lie on, 'They lie like swine upon the ground'.

There was no segregation in Newgate in the daytime and therefore women and girls were in real danger in such a place. On the one hand there was every chance that a woman could find someone to make her pregnant if she wanted to 'plead her belly', i.e. prove that she was pregnant (which meant that she would avoid execution), but there was also a good chance that a woman prisoner could be raped in such anarchic and disgraceful conditions.

It isn't widely known that the prisoners were sometimes used as guinea pigs for medical experiments. The first British innoculations took place using Newgate prisoners and other medical experiments were performed on prisoners in return for reductions in prison sentences.

Mr Akerman, the Keeper of the prison and an unusually humane person compared to others before him, appeared before a House of Parliament Committee in 1779, and admitted that many prisoners 'had died broken-hearted'.

When Casanova (yes, that one) lived in London he spent some time in Newgate for an assault and said that he had felt 'as if he was in one of the most horrible circles of Dante's hell'.

DANIEL GONZALEZ – AN OLD BAILEY TRIAL

'I wanted to be Freddy Krueger for a day.'

Not many serial killers have been more disturbed than Daniel Gonzalez. Back in 2004 Gonzalez was just 24 when, completely at random, he killed four people and tried to kill two others in a three day whirlwind of extreme psychotic violence.

Although he lived outside London, three of his four murder victims were attacked in north London, Kevin Molloy in Tottenham, and retired couple Derek and Jean Robinson in Highgate. All were stabbed multiple times and had their throats cut. He had also bitten off one of Derek Robinson's fingers.

After his arrest Gonzalez said he had planned to kill at least 10 people and had been under the control of 'voices'.

Before he went on the final rampage Gonzalez, who was a drinker and drugger, had been running around naked near his house trying to smash his own nose by diving headfirst onto a bin-lid. He told psychiatrists before his suicide, 'I wanted to degrade myself, self-degradation made me feel better'.

On 15 September 2004, armed with a steak knife, Gonzalez launched his first attack on a 61-year-old man out walking with his wife. The attack failed because, although injured, the man fought back. Gonzalez then apologised and significantly said, 'I'm a schizophrenic, I can't help it'. Six years before he had spent 7 months in a psychiatric unit after being diagnosed as schizophrenic.

Later the same day near Brighton he killed a Mrs Harding because she 'looked like a schoolteacher'. Later he wrote in a note, 'It felt really, really good … a proper bloodbath … One of the best things I've done in my life … I will be a serial killer'.

Two days later in Tottenham he stabbed Kevin Molloy to death with two knives and within three hours he had also butchered Derek and Jean Robinson, the Highgate couple. Although covered in blood from another abortive murder attempt in between, a shop had sold Gonzalez a 12-inch kitchen knife which he used on the couple. When a shocked decorator discovered their bodies, along with blood all over the walls, and then saw a naked Gonzalez, Gonzalez reportedly said, 'Sorry about this, mate' before making his escape. Gonzalez said that he felt after the murder of the couple that 'I had washed all the crap out of my life … I felt like a superhero'. In a terrible irony, Derek Robinson had been an important volunteer for an organisation which tried to improve the lives of tortured teenagers.

Compounding the terror, during the attacks Gonzalez wore an icehockey mask similar to the one worn by fictional serial killer character Jason Voorhees from the *Friday the 13th* slasher films. He also idolised Voorhees' 'rival' the serial killer character Freddy Krueger from the *Nightmare on Elm Street* films.

After his arrest Gonzalez assaulted a number of policemen (he had previously written in a note, 'I will kill as many old bill (police) as I can').

The sadness underlying the horrendous violence can be seen in this statement to the police by Gonzalez,

> *'I didn't want to grow up … I'm going to kill myself. I'm a little baby and I don't feel very well'.*

On the other hand it is hard to sympathise too much with someone who goes onto Friends Reunited, as Gonzalez did, leaving a message on his school's page saying that at least now people who knew him could say they'd been to school with someone famous!

Even psychiatrists and guards at Broadmoor (who are pretty unshockable because they have seen it all before) were shocked by Gonzalez' crazed determination to kill himself. He tried many times to bite though the veins in his wrists before finally succeeded in killing himself in 2007 by slashing his wrists with a broken CD case. He was 27.

His grandmother called him 'the fifth victim' and his mother too feels her clearly massively disturbed son never got the help he needed. Before her son's murder spree she had written a prophetic plea for help, 'Does Daniel have to murder or be murdered before he gets the treatment he so badly needs?'

My favourite Old Bailey anecdote (warning – bad language coming up, but necessary for the story) features a Cockney prisoner who was sentenced to death by the judge and reacted to the spectacle of the judge's with slow deliberation as he donned the black cap (the meant to be terrifying ritual before declaring a death sentence), by equally deliberately yawning slowly and confiding to the courtroom: 'Gloomy fucker ain't he?'

9) Jack the Ripper Part 2: 9 King's Bench Walk, Inner Temple

Tube: Blackfriars.

Travel to Blackfriars underground station. Exit and cross the road in front of you. Turn right and walk up New Bridge Street and in less than a minute you will find Tudor Street on the left. Walk into Tudor Street and continue to the end of that street where you will find a little archway which should be open during daylight hours (it shuts at midnight). The small street immediately on the other side of the archway is Kings Bench Walk and if you turn left you will find No. 9 in just a few seconds.

SOMETHING WICKED THIS WAY COMES

Montague John Druitt, my Ripper suspect, worked here at 9 King's Bench Walk, Inner Temple. The actual house is still here and, externally at least, can be viewed in the daytime but the lawyers who work there will *not* be happy if you knock at the door, so please do not do that. People do not have a right to walk through this Inner Temple lawyers' area but the lawyers permit it so long as they are quiet. Incidentally, the Temple church (page 105) is only about 5 minutes' walk away from here.

Perhaps moving away from where the actual Ripper murders were performed in the East End (but where little remains as it was at the time) can help to cast a different and fresh light on those murders. However, it is important to restate at the outset what was said in Part 1 (page 73), that nearly all the evidence in the Ripper case is purely circumstantial.

There are no murder weapons (although occasionally weapons, diaries or letters seem to turn up in the care of people writing Ripper books…). There is no useful DNA available from either suspects or victims. At this remove in time there is no longer a perpetrator at large, no witnesses, and no investigators with first-hand knowledge of the crimes. Everyone connected, including Jack the Ripper himself, died long ago. Anyone who could have had an authentic contemporary memory of 'the autumn of terror' would now be around 133 years old at the youngest and of course there is no-one alive that old.

All we have now is the jigsaw puzzle. My best fit to the Jack the Ripper jigsaw puzzle is a man called Montague John Druitt. He is well-known as a suspect and the following list is a round-up of the circumstantial evidence and a little bit of new information. First, some basics.

Montague John Druitt was born in 1857 into an upper middle class family in Wimborne in Dorset. He went to Winchester College and then New College in Oxford. After graduation he may have done a year's medicine but he then switched to law and studied here at the Inner Temple in London from 1882–1885. He then practised as a lawyer his base being at 9 King's Bench Walk. His father died in 1885. His mother was sent to a mental asylum in July 1888. Five prostitutes were brutally murdered in or around Whitechapel between 31 August and 9 November 1888. Montague committed suicide at the end of 1888 and his body was pulled from the Thames on the last day of the year.

ANATOMY OF A RIPPER SUSPECT

1) Like a bolt from the blue, Montague John Druitt was named in a 1894 Metropolitan Police report as a major Jack the Ripper suspect, and although two other men were mentioned in the report (both lower class jailbirds), Druitt is clearly the favoured suspect in that report.

2) The 1894 police report naming Druitt hints very strongly that certain unnamed members of the Druitt family had been secretly in touch with the

police and had themselves stated that they thought Montague was Jack the Ripper.

3) Montague was 31 at the time of the murders – serial killers on average begin killing in their late twenties to early thirties.

4) The Druitt family had a marked history of insanity. His mother was confined to a mental asylum at the time of the murders. Her mother had committed suicide, one of Montague's sisters committed suicide and Montague himself committed suicide.

5) After Montague committed suicide there were no more Jack the Ripper murders.

6) Two years *before* the police report mentioned in 1) above, Dorset MP Henry Farquharson unexpectedly revealed to the media that he believed Jack the Ripper had been the son of a surgeon and that he had committed suicide after the last murder. He said he could not say more (implying he knew more) because of a fear of libel. All this points to Montague John Druitt of the famous medical family, the Druitts of Wimborne in Dorset.

7) Many family members were doctors and surgeons. Montague's father William was a well-known surgeon and his uncle Robert was a famous surgeon and author of an all-time classic medical text book, 'the standard work for every trainee surgeon for more than half a century'. They both specialised in obstetrics. 'Obstetrics is the care of the pregnant mother and her baby pre- and perinatally. In many areas it overlaps with gynaecology'.

However, Montague himself, after a bright academic beginning, faded badly and only got a third class degree at university. He gave up studying medicine after just one year. Could this failure, in the light of the elder males' golden successes, have helped prey on his mind? Also what was the effect on Montague's fragile mind, in a household clearly a prey to insanity, of all those medical books with their typically Victorian sternly prohibitive chapters on sexuality and graphic cutaway diagrams of female anatomy? Those Victorian cutaway diagrams with depictions of sharp medical instruments probing, slicing and hacking the female reproductive organs can look disturbingly similar to assaults.

In his classic surgeon's textbook Robert Druitt admonishes that 'perfect chastity' is necessary. Elsewhere he promotes 'the repression of vice in any open form'. Could Montague's unsound mind have taken this as encouragement to act against prostitutes in his own unique way?

8) Montague only completed one year of medicine before switching to studying law. However, this medical background would obviously have helped with the organ removals. Having only one year's experience would also help

explain why the organ removals indicated to most observers some degree of medical knowledge but not necessarily expertise.

9) Montague's mother was committed to a local asylum five weeks before the Ripper murders began. This sad development is what is called a stressor: many serial killers have reported that they struck when something went majorly wrong in their life such as breaking up with a partner, losing a job, etc. His mother being diagnosed as mad and actually confined to an asylum would have been devastating to Montague and a very potent stressor.

10) Druitt's location at 9 King's Bench Walk in the Inner Temple off Fleet Street means he was living literally metres away from newspaper offices that received letters purporting to come from the killer.

11) Connecting Whitechapel to Mum's mental asylum in Clapton was just a single road in a straight line. It would have made sense for Montague to have visited his mother by going from Blackfriars to Whitechapel on the Metropolitan District line, then getting a bus or tram up the long road to the mental asylum. There were no cars or taxis in those days. This could have been the original motivation to explore Whitechapel.

12) Druitt was a good cricketer and had come third in a cricket ball throwing contest. He therefore had very good wrist strength which would have been vital in the blitz attack strangulations.

13) Was the fifth murder's timing, occurring on the Lord Mayor's day, the City's biggest annual occasion, just coincidental? That big occasion, 9 November 1888, was ruined by newspaper boys shouting 'Horrible murder, horrible murder'. Druitt had only to walk for 90 seconds to be on Fleet Street to observe this.

14) People sometimes say that Druitt would have been hard-pressed to be in certain places after the murders. The example very often given is we know he was playing a cricket match a few hours after second victim Annie Chapman was murdered. Some people say it's unlikely that someone would brutally murder someone and then play a cricket match just a few hours later. This displays a misunderstanding of the nature of an alibi. The ideal alibi in this situation is that you *do* turn up for the cricket match people are expecting you to play in, no matter how tired you are. If you miss the match, people may wonder why.

A certain gangster once went to a nightclub, made sure he was seen by many people, popped out a back door and killed someone. That is the ideal alibi: you make it seem that you couldn't have done something but you actually could have (just).

15) Let's take a look at the language of the Ripper communications. Even if you only take the notorious George Lusk 'kidney' letter as authentic (Jack the

Ripper sent Whitechapel vigilante committee leader Lusk a letter bragging about his depravity accompanied by half the fourth prostitute's left kidney), then it seems obvious that the writer is faking an Irish accent (the author of this book is Irish). Also the wording in the Lusk letter reads like someone of an upper class trying to imitate (badly) someone of a lower class. Why? Perhaps to try to deflect from his own English accent and upper middle class background and to make trouble for a demonised minority group at that time, the Irish.

Exactly the same motivation could apply to the notorious Goulston Street graffiti (see page 73). This ambivalent piece of writing could be from a Jewish person or it could be blaming the Jews for the Ripper murders. Some writers (myself included) believe that far from being Jewish himself Jack the Ripper was deflecting attention as far away as possible from himself and trying to stir up trouble in a devilishly clever way. This after all was an East End of London that had seen mass immigration of Jews in the previous twenty years to escape persecutions abroad. What better way to create a smokescreen and cause trouble than to perform grotesquely horrible murders in the area then leave a message saying the Jews, another demonised minority, were responsible? Notice also that the grafitti was written in chalk. Only schoolteachers habitually carry chalk around – Druitt was a part-time schoolteacher in Blackheath, South London.

16) There is a curious 'coincidence' about two of the murder streets and two streets around King's Bench Walk. To approach King's Bench Walk from Fleet Street you pass through Mitre Court. The fourth victim was found dead in Mitre Square. At the back entrance to King's Bench Walk, where Druitt's House was, was a street called Dorset Rise. The fifth victim was found butchered in Dorset Street.

17) Let's look at the name Jack the Ripper itself. Why call himself Jack? Possible answer: John (as in Montague John) and Jack were interchangeable. In addition, right beside the lawyer's area was Fleet Street which had a much-visited and much-loved sight, the famous ancient clock of St Dunstan's with a bell struck quarterly by a 'Jack', a human figure with a hammer.

18) The Lusk letter was signed 'From Hell'. There is the obvious demonic reference here but there may also be a knowing pun since Montague had attended Winchester school and a particular piece of ground at the school was known in school slang by teachers and pupils alike as 'Hell'.

19) One of the most detailed witness descriptions is by Sergeant Stephen White and his description is remarkably close to Druitt, he said the man was '5 feet 10 inches tall, and was about 33 years old, shabbily dressed, and with

a long, thin face, delicate nostrils, jet-black hair, brilliant eyes and long, snow-white hands and fingers'.

20) A rumour came from somewhere that Prince Albert Victor, the Duke of Clarence, might have been involved in the murders. Druitt's face is spookily like Clarence's – they both have a remarkably languid facial appearance. You can easily imagine someone seeing the one hurrying along in the dark, and getting confused with the other.

21) At the time of the murders, blood-stained clothing was found between Whitechapel and the Temple district, at Ludgate Hill, 5 minutes away from Druitt's King's Bench Walk address. Also, at one point the police secretly kept a close watch on people going to mass in St Paul's Cathedral (as Druitt would have been expected to do on occasion) in connection with the murders. In fact at the time police sources said they regarded this surveillance as the best hope of an arrest. St Paul's at the top of Ludgate Hill was about 10 minutes away from 9 King's Bench Walk. Both facts skew the probable location of the murderer unexpectedly away from the East End and towards the Inner Temple and Druitt's base.

22) Basil Thompson corroborated the official suspicion that 'in the belief of the police he was a man who committed suicide in the Thames at the end of 1888' and who 'had been at some time a medical student'. Again this points to Druitt.

There is much more to be said about Jack the Ripper and Montague John Druitt, but in a book covering many aspects of the dark side of London, and not just Jack the Ripper, I have to stop there.

THREE RIPPER MYTHS NAILED

1) **Assertion:** *Jack the Ripper was a sadistic serial killer.*

Reality: *It may be counter-intuitive but Jack the Ripper was not a sadistic serial killer. He was terrifyingly brutal, cold and evil but, technically, he was not particularly sadistic. He killed the prostitutes quickly. He did not inflict pain in small lingering doses over a period of time instead he sought annihilation of the victim. He is the destroyer type.*

2) **Assertion:** *Jack the Ripper was a member of the Royal family at the time or perhaps their doctor.*

Reality: *Stephen Knights's 1970s book* Jack the Ripper: The Final Solution *(Bounty Books; Revised edition, 2000), seems initially impressive in weaving* *a tale of supposed frolics by Prince Albert Victor, Victoria's grandson, with a woman from the lower classes leading to an illegitimate child. Mary Kelly, the fifth and final Ripper victim supposedly knows of that child, leading to her murder and the murders of the other prostitutes by the Queen's doctor, William Gull, and others. The problem is that it just doesn't add up. People didn't live where they are supposed to have lived, buildings didn't exist where the book says they were, etc. It is a (best-selling) tale.*

3) **Assertion:** *In her* Portrait of a Killer: Jack The Ripper – Case Closed *(Berkley True Crime, 2003), novelist Patricia Cornwell claims that Walter Sickert, a well-known, successful Victorian professional painter, was Jack the Ripper.*

   Reality: *The book is very lavish with assertions but spends remarkably little time backing them up. Quite apart from that, can anyone reading my book name me one successfully creative individual who was a serial killer? It is not a coincidence that people who are successful creatively aren't serial killers. Serial killers are non-achievers, they are empty hate machines. Creative types can actually use their art to exorcise their demons (and Sickert may be doing exactly that in some of his more macabre paintings – but that's all). If the logic that messed-up art equals serial killer is followed through then what are we to make of Francis Bacon or Damien Hirst?*

10) St Andrew-by-the-Wardrobe

St Andrew-by-the-Wardrobe, St Andrew's Hill, London EC4V 5DE. Tel: 020 7329 3632. The church building and the Chapel of St Ann are normally open for visitors Monday to Friday from 10a.m.–4 p.m. Tube: Blackfriars.

Leave Blackfriars tube station and walk for 10 seconds round to the right. Cross the traffic lights in front. Queen Victoria Street is on the right. This 300-year-old church is just 5 minutes' walk along Queen Victoria Street, on the left-hand side. If you go this way you pass a street on the left called St Andrew's Hill but keep walking and shortly afterwards you can enter the church on the left by walking up 25 steps. If this entrance is not open you can go back to St Andrew's Hill and walk up it for about 30 seconds and then you will find another entrance to the church on the right-hand side. Either before or after visiting the church you might want to visit the pleasant pub in St Andrew's Hill called The Cockpit; it's worth a visit in its own right as the last place in London where bird-fighting was legal, plus it has decent food and friendly managers.

APPARITION

The church of St Andrew-by-the-Wardrobe is reputedly haunted and all I can say is that I personally have experience of something very strange here. I have always been open to the possibility that ghosts might exist, whatever they are, and have had the attitude that it's probably safest to assume that, as Horatio is informed by Hamlet in Shakespeare's *Hamlet*, 'There are more things in heaven and earth, Horatio, than are dreamt of in your philosophy'. However, I personally do not go around seeing ghosts.

With one exception.

This is the only place where I think I have seen an apparition not just once but three times, and always in the same place.

St Andrew-by-the-Wardrobe was the last City church built by Christopher Wren. It was completed in 1695, so it is externally over 300 years old (although the inside is from 1959 because it was blitzed in World War Two and reduced to a shell, then rebuilt). It is not a beautiful church but it is an important one for me because of its Shakespearean memorials and connections (my other great love, apart from the dark side of London, is William Shakespeare). It is fairly ironic, given that I do a well-known horror walk called 'The Blood and Tears Walk', that I visit this particular church not because it is reputedly haunted, but only because of its Shakespeare memorials.

This 'thing' I have seen has always appeared in the same place, just to the left of the platform halfway up the staircase which is ahead and to your left when you enter from Great Victoria Street, or directly ahead of you and to the right if you enter from the St Andrew's Hill entrance.

This little platform has at its back a wall with a plaque to a church warden and his family. On the right-hand side is a painting of the local area on a second wall at right angles to the first one. From the platform the staircase twists up to the left to a balcony from which you can observe the main body of the church. The balcony has a little gallery behind it but there are no stairs at the other end so it is a dead end.

What's really bizarre is that every time I have seen this apparition (a word Shakespeare invented) I have actually been doing my 'Shakespeare City Walk' for people. This has led to the further complication of me trying to continue to talk about Shakespeare on those particular occasions without betraying either amazement or nervousness or excitement.

Why have the others doing my Shakespeare walk with me apparently not seen anything on the occasions when I have seen something? Possibly because they were directly behind and below me, the leader, as I began to climb the stairs and I was blocking their view. Or possibly because they just weren't looking in the right direction; or perhaps even one or two people over the years have thought they saw something but distrusted their senses or decided not to talk about it. Or maybe only certain individuals can see such things (whether they want to or not).

What was the 'thing' that I saw?

First, I have always been aware that the air appears to 'swim' here more than is normal, and I have noticed this appears to be a characteristic (for me at least) of places where either bad/intense/supernatural things have happened, but the first time I actually saw anything strange wasn't until I had already been doing my 'Shakespeare City Walk' for some 6–7 years.

Doing the tour one day and entering the church as usual, I was just at the bottom of the staircase when I suddenly became aware with my peripheral vision that there appeared to be some sort of cloud/shape further up ahead and to the left. This cloud/shape suddenly made a very fast and distinctive movement further on up to the left. As I have already said there is a balcony up there with a gallery behind it but it is otherwise a dead end.

The first time I saw this 'something' I clearly remember continuing to talk to the people on the tour about the Shakespeare memorials in the church while visually confirming to myself that there was nowhere for anyone to hide once you checked the balcony and the gallery behind it.

In this kind of situation, when you are confronted with something unknown, your first instinct is still to assume that you have somehow seen a human, even though the behaviour is not human-like.

I would describe the motion of the 'thing' as being (it's the only way I can adequately describe it) a bit like the motion of a fish which has been basking in a pool but suddenly whisks away at someone's approach.

My girlfriend clearly remembers this first occasion because when I came home that night and talked about it she was a bit frightened by my bewilderment and amazement since she had never heard me talk about such an experience before. I told her I thought I had seen a bit of fabric and a hint of face.

A couple of weeks later, after almost convincing myself that it had been a trick of the light, the same thing happened. A couple of months later, the same. Each time I thought I saw a fragment more fabric and face although indistinct.

I did some research and found that St Andrew-by-the-Wardrobe features in some books on 'haunted London'. I had not known this. At the bottom of the stairs is a huge disconnected bell; this has reputedly sometimes rung by itself if someone dies connected to the church from which the bell originally came.

Incidentally, the experience was not horrifying. The temperature did not suddenly plunge à la *Exorcist* and although I was a little freaked out I was not very afraid (although I wouldn't fancy spending a night alone in this church). If anything it felt like I had disturbed *it*, whatever it was. I clearly remember that on the first occasion I felt like I had intruded on it almost as if it had been musing and then realised a bit late that it had been seen and had to go.

If anyone goes to the church to see whether they feel/see anything I strongly encourage zero expectations (it's always best) but to be sensitive to the quality of the air and also to be very aware of your peripheral vision rather than what is straight ahead of you. If you do see something, or perhaps more accurately if you become aware of something (and like I say it's a big if), it seems to happen fleetingly and almost out of the field of vision.

11) John Wilkes – Hellfire Club

Tube: Temple or Chancery Lane.

About 10–12 minutes away from either Temple or Chancery Lane tube stations, half-way up Fetter Lane, where it converges with New Fetter Lane, on a little 'island' surrounded by traffic, is a statue of radical English politician John Wilkes in his eighteenth-Century costume. The statue was erected in 1988 and the writing on the base proudly declares 'A champion of English freedom'.

This is the only squinting statue in London (true to the fact that Wilkes had a pronounced squint) and it is here because Wilkes lived near here at one point.

Behind the statue, 30 seconds away at 108 Fetter Lane is the White Swan, a highly rated gastropub.

The 'Hellfire Caves', mentioned in the text below, are in West Wycombe, about half an hour's train ride from London (Chiltern line from Marylebone station), and are a thriving tourist attraction. More details at www.hellfirecaves.co.uk.

DANCING WITH MR D

Most people who buy this book will probably have a fair degree of cynicism about human behaviour already, and might be inclined to be especially cynical about the behaviour of rulers. Even some of the cynics though might have difficulty believing the following and yet it is true.

If in say 1762 you had been able to attend Parliament on a Friday afternoon you might have observed the Prime Minister Bute, the Chancellor of the Exchequer

Sir Francis Dashwood, the Lord Mayor, the Earl of Sandwich (John Montagu) plus John Wilkes debating with others.

Probably nothing in that scene would have struck you as unusual.

However, could you have transported yourself the next night by boat from London to Marlow, arriving at midnight at the eerie ruins of an ancient and consecrated Abbey called Medmenham (pronounced Mednam) on the bank of the Thames, 6 miles from Sir Francis Dashwood's West Wycombe mansion, you might well have found the same cast of characters, but in a very different setting and doing very different things.

You entered the Abbey under the words 'Fay ce que vouldras' ('Do whatever you want'), non-coincidentally the same precept as Aleister Crowley's 'Do what thou wilt'.

In addition to the previous men you might also have spotted in their white robes in the gardens or in the Abbey's penitential cells William Hogarth (the famous painter who appears elsewhere in this book), Benjamin Franklin, Colonel Francis Charteris (known as the Rapemaster general) and George Selwyn.

A brief look at Selwyn and Sandwich's predilections will give you an idea of the mentality of the Friars of St Francis of Wycombe's Hellfire Club: Selwyn had a fetish for attending executions (he once travelled to Paris to watch a man executed by being pulled apart by horses), and paying undertakers to examine corpses. Montagu, the Earl of Sandwich created 'the sandwich' so he would not have to leave the gambling table during all-night gambling sessions.

The participating men at Medmenham were almost all from the aristocracy. Most of them had money (although some had gambled it away) and they were bored and cynical. They had contempt for the old order of things and a kind of nihilism, and people referred to them as 'the Hell-rakes'.

In other words the British government had within it at that time some 10–15 members (at least) of a scandalous secret society whose activities included orgies as well as dubious darker rites.

The difficulty in writing about them at this remove is how to disentangle how much of their behaviour precisely was 'rake' and how much did genuinely partake of 'hell'.

On the 'rake' side some of the 'monks' behaviour at the Abbey is reminiscent of modern era 'frat-boy' drunken partying, and sex was always a major part of the lure of this secret society. Prostitutes by the hundred were paid to cater to the whims of jaded libertines who constantly needed ever newer and more outrageous stimulations. First they had orgies. Then ordinary orgies somehow palled and a new twist was needed. Why not spice them up by adding in some half-sisters and even a mother or two of the participants? The hell-rake attitude to women was very questionable: they tended to buy, use, and throw them away like garbage.

On the 'hell' side rituals flirted with, and teetered on the edge of, satanism and every so often fell over. The very first meeting of the Order of Knights of West Wycombe had taken place on Walpurgis Night, the night of witches and unhallowed things. Wilkes once frightened Sandwich half to death by unleashing a baboon in the darkness after Sandwich had been flirting with a satanic ceremony. When certain members were in the mood, activities could have a more sinister edge. They were fond of blasphemy: there were 12 'apostles', Dashwood being Christ himself. Black masses were rumoured which used a naked woman's body as the altar. Upside-down crucifixes and black candles were whispered of. Magical and powerful herbs were used. There was Hocus Pocus (that phrase comes from blasphemous ceremonies in which a host is raised and the words 'Hic est corpus' or 'This is the Body (of Christ)' spoken.) The full details are frustratingly scanty however.

Under Dashwood's mansion in West Wycombe (beside which is a six-sided family mausoleum which again keeps up the occult vibes connected to Dashwood and his disciples), are caves, now publicly accessible, where meetings of the Hellfire Club probably also took place. Deep underground you cross 'the river Styx' to reach the Inner Temple which is the hardest part of the caves to reach and would presumably have had the most secret activities.

The club kept most of its secrets but the whole complex is creepy and still well worth a visit.

12) Mithraic Temple: Temple Court, Queen Victoria Street

Tube: Mansion House.

N.B. The Temple of Mithras, formerly at the above location, opposite the ultra-modern gray and green HSBC building, is in storage now until at least 2016. At that time it is going to be relocated by Bloomberg to its original Roman London location on Walbrook, close to Bank underground station, and there will be a new exit from Bank station leading to the relocated, bigger installation in the new Bloomberg HQ building, complete with better-presented information about the cult. Bloomberg intend to make the temple more faithful to how it would originally have been.

COULD HAVE BEEN A CONTENDER

Not far from St Paul's, practically in its long shadow, was until recently a small wind-swept, little-visited monument. It was the butchered remains of a temple of a vanquished cult that was once a rival to the Christianity St Paul's Cathedral amply glorifies, but which Christianity itself persecuted and finally destroyed. The cult was devoted to a god called Mithras, and ironically the adjective most attached to him was 'invincible'.

The poorly presented remains of the London temple, known as a Mithraeum, did not feature in any list of the most-visited tourist attractions in London. The occasional tourist wandered by, wondered what the pile of stones was, and then wandered off again.

Mithraism is the worship of Mithras, a sun god. There was a similar god with a very similar name, Mitra, in Persia but the connections are obscure. The version under discussion here is the later Roman Empire cult. Cults by definition are not part of the mainstream, but for 300 years from AD 90 to AD 391 (after which Christianised Rome banned all pagan cults) thousands across every part of the Roman Empire worshipped Mithras. The cult was very popular among soldiers, slaves, and ordinary freed men particularly clerks or 'civil servants' and it certainly was a potential rival to Christianity in the West.

Shopkeepers felt an affinity to Mithras because he was the God of contracts. Soldiers on the other hand were probably attracted to the cult's masculine – even macho – image. No women were allowed in the cult and the god's physical strength was emphasised. In addition army life meant that soldiers were already comfortable with discipline and ritual and familiar with communal meals. Also, to join the cult and rise in its hierarchy you had to be willing to undergo initiation rites.

The main feature of the religion was venerating the bull-killing god in Mithraeum (temples or caves) such as this one in London. Participants wore animal masks and had to undergo sometimes gruelling initiations not for the faint-hearted. There were seven levels of hierarchy in the cult and indeed the number seven had special significance overall for the cult. There were seven pillars, for example, in the underground chamber. There would have been a bull-killing sculpture in the Temple showing Mithras killing the bull and thereby bringing forth new life. A dog and snake were often depicted, allies to Mithras, while a scorpion would represent unhelpful forces.

One initiation ceremony may have been to lie in a trench – the outline of the London Temple trench is clear – while a bull was slaughtered above you, drenching you in a literal bloodbath. This was called the taurobolium. Other initiation ceremonies or ordeals involved experiencing hunger, extremes of hot and cold and being confronted with danger. Temples sometimes have narrow benches right next to where fires would have burnt and so the initiate may well have been asked to sit very close to the fire for some time. There are also references to another ordeal in which the man's hands were bound, he was blindfolded and required to jump over a trench of water. Temples sometimes had ordeal pits in which the initiate would have been placed for some time to give the feeling of being buried alive.

Other aspects of the ritual involved brightly coloured red and yellow walls, wavering and flickering light effects and flowing water: the original site of the London Temple before it was moved was originally where the river Walbrook flows, close to modern day Bank underground station.

There were sudden revelations and the reciting of secret words (one we now know of was 'Nama' or 'Hail' in Persian), the learning of secret symbols and signs of cult membership, plus the ringing of bells and making of sudden loud disorientating noises. You could call it psychedelic disorientation. There is a Masonic feel to some of this but this cult came first.

Some of what follows is supposition because the whole point of cults is that they are private affairs, but apparently you worked through the seven grades as follows (St Jerome records their names) with seven being the highest grade: 1) *Corax, Corux or Corvex* (raven or crow) 2) *Nymphus, Nymphobus* (male bride) 3) *Miles* (soldier) 4) *Leo* (lion) 5) *Perses* (Persian) 6) *Heliodromus* (sun-runner) and finally 7) *Pater* (father).

Different grades had different rituals and obligations. For example, when a member reached the third grade of *Miles* or soldier he was offered a crown on the point of a sword but once he placed it on his head he was to immediately remove it and offer it to Mithras. The Lion or fourth grade was the first of the senior grades and could not touch water ritually.

Some Christians took the opportunity to characterise Mithraism as dark and evil because of the rituals in caves and underground locations. Some Christians also despised Mithraism because it also featured a holy meal and a Eucharistic display which Christianity found profane. Mithraic burials took place on the East to West axis like Christian ones do and, worst of all and not to be endured, both Christianity and Mithraism believed in a God who was born from a virgin on 25 December.

The London temple, and eventually the other ones in Britain (all connected with Roman army sites), was destroyed in the fourth century. It is interesting that before its destruction, the Temple of Mithras, a cult which emphasised asceticism rather than indulgence, appears to have been hijacked by the cult of Bacchus, the god of drinking.

The excavator of the Temple of Mithras in 1954, a famous London archaeologist called Grimes who spent two years of his life on the dig, said about the way the stones were shunted to a different site and then again to the current site "The result is visually meaningless as a reconstruction of a Mithraeum".

Has this disrespect been an unconscious (or even conscious!) way of destroying the memory of the power of a once important religion? A bit like how execution destroys the body of a victim and then dismemberment attempts to destroy their spirit also so they cannot then be resurrected whole?

MADAME TUSSAUDS CHAMBER OF HORRORS

Tube: Baker Street.

The Chamber of Horrors has been an integral part of Madame Tussauds waxworks collection since its inception in Paris in the late eighteenth century. Mme Tussaud brought the collection to England in 1802 and it toured the country before settling on its current location on Marylebone Road (near Baker Street station) in 1884.

Here are some lesser-known facts about the collection.

1) 'Acid-bath killer' John Haigh (see page 133) had a penchant for taking girlfriends to see the Madam

Tussauds Chamber of Horrors exhibition. Peter Kurten, 1920s Dusseldorf serial killer, was also fascinated by the Chamber of Horrors and so too was one of the twentieth century's most notorious serial killers – Peter Sutcliffe, the 'Yorkshire Ripper'. In the last few hours of his life Haigh made a gift to Madam Tussauds (which they accepted) – a set of his clothes for the Chamber of Horrors. He wanted his mannequin there to look just right in his green suit, green socks, and red tie with green squares. Haigh specified that the trousers were to be pressed and that an inch of shirt cuff was to be showing.

2) In 1820 a model of Cato Street conspirator (page 31) Arthur Thistlewood's head was shown for a year or so.

3) Punch magazine popularised the phrase 'Chamber of Horrors' in a critical article about the exhibition. Punch also described the lure of the Chamber of Horrors as 'A sort of fascination in the horrible'.

4) The Baker Street site opened in 1884 just a few years before the Jack the Ripper murders of 1888 but Jack the Ripper was never modelled for the Chamber of Horrors. The reason was that Jack's identity remains unknown, and Tussauds has always stuck strictly to modelling the actual faces of criminals.

5) Amelia Dyer (page 66), baby-farmer, was a popular waxwork in the Madame Tussauds Chamber of Horrors even into the late 1960s.

6) In 1910 Dr Crippen killed his wife in favour of life with his mistress. The Crippen model's head split in two in the 1931 London earthquake!

6 SOUTH-WEST LONDON

1) Coleherne pub (now called The Pembroke)

The Pembroke, 261 Old Brompton Road. Opening times: Monday to Sunday 12p.m.–12a.m. Food serving times: Monday to Saturday 12p.m.–4.30p.m. and 6p.m.–10.30p.m. Sunday 12p.m.– 9.30p.m. Tube: West Brompton.

Go to West Brompton underground station. Walk outside and turn right onto Old Brompton Road. Keep walking, past Brompton Cemetery on the right, for about 5–6 minutes or so until you come to The Pembroke on the right-hand side at 261 Old Brompton Road.

PSYCHOPATHS' PLAYGROUND

(NB this chapter description refers to when the building was called The Coleherne and has no reference to the current renamed pub under different management.)

The Pembroke has been a gastropub at 261 Old Brompton Road since January 2009, but in its former incarnation the building used to be known as the Coleherne. The Coleherne is the only London pub known to have been frequented by three serial killers, and at least two of them killed people they actually picked up from the pub.

The Coleherne had one of the longest-running histories in London as a gay venue, having been defiantly gay since the late 1950s. By the time of the 1970s it had become very well-known as London's first 'leather bar', a place for gay devotees of leather to meet and, if they felt like it, to have anonymous sex in backrooms. Some internationally famous people went there for fun but three people who later became famous as serial killers also went there, and at least two of them used it as a cruising ground for victims. The serial killers are Denis Nilsen, Michael Lupo and Colin Ireland.

DENNIS NILSEN

Nilsen is dealt with elsewhere in this book (page 7) but according to the best biography of Nilsen, (*Killing For Company: The Case of Dennis Nilsen* by Brian

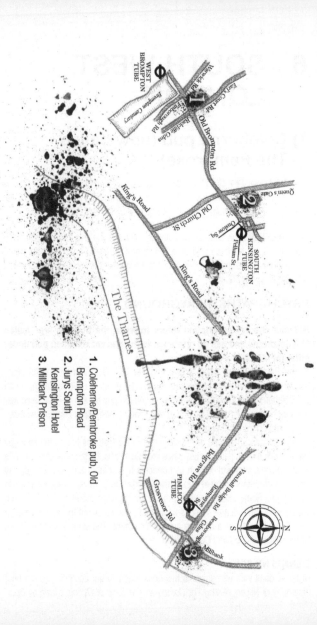

1. Coleherne/Pembroke pub, Old
   Brompton Road
2. Jurys South
   Kensington Hotel
3. Millbank Prison

Masters, Arrow, New edition 1995) the Coleherne was the first gay pub that Nilsen got to know in London. Beyond this it has not been proven that any of his victims were picked up from here, but that he knew the pub and had been there is indisputable.

MICHAEL LUPO

Thirty-three-year-old Italian Michael Lupo very definitely had two sides. One side was the chatty, handsome manager of the Brompton Road branch of Yves St Laurent. This Michael was known to many well-known people and had slept with some of them, of both sexes.

The other Michael was a sadistic, perverted sex killer capable of biting a man's tongue off while murdering him.

Lupo picked up his first murder victim at the Coleherne in March 1987. Five nights previously he had picked up a different man at the Coleherne and strangled him into unconsciousness with a scarf, but this time 36-year-old James Burns was strangled to death with the scarf. When his body was found it was noticed that Burns's chest had been savagely bitten and, even worse, his tongue had been bitten off. Lupo was clearly rampantly sadistic. Following his arrest after four murders, Lupo confessed without any emotion. It turned out that Lupo had AIDS and the police wondered if one possible motivation for the murders might have been some kind of warped revenge attack on the scene that had given him the disease. Lupo would not confirm this, merely claiming that he felt he had 'been used and abused in the past it was just anger (sic)'. Lupo died in prison from AIDS in 1995.

Derek Jarman, internationally famous filmmaker and artist, revealed in his diaries that he had had sex with Lupo.

COLIN IRELAND

'I have always dreamed of doing the perfect murder.'

39-year-old Colin Ireland was a tall, well-built Southend-based ex-soldier. An illegitimate child and troubled teenager, in December 1992 Ireland found himself in his late thirties living in a hostel with two failed marriages behind him. Nothing seemed to be going right in his life, so Ireland made a New Year's resolution that in 1993 he would finally become the serial killer he had wanted to be for some time.

Ireland picked up all five of his victims at the Coleherne pub. He later told the police that he thought killing gay men would lead to less sympathy for the victims than if he had killed women.

Inside the Coleherne in March 1993, the first victim, Peter Walker, accidentally spilled a drink over Ireland and then asked Ireland to punish him.

Ireland decided he would do just that and at his house Walker was asphyxiated with a plastic bag.

Ireland killed five men in just over three months in houses all over London. The other four men were strangled with a ligature. The victims had thought they were going to be taking part in consensual sadomasochistic practises but once they were immobilised they were tortured and eventually killed.

Ireland told the police that he knew he had to kill four to be classed as a serial killer. In fact he was wrong because three would have been enough to achieve the classification.

Thankfully, Ireland was not quite as smart as he thought he was and the perfect murder eluded him, but he did get away with it for a while. Ironically, it was his pestering of the police in phone calls, and his revelations of various details which only the killer could know, that made them link the previously unconnected deaths and mount the investigation which led to his capture. In December 1993, exactly a year after his New Year's resolution, Ireland received a life sentence.

Some people think that the Coleherne never quite got over those murders. In March 2012 Ireland died of natural causes.

The Nag's Head, 53 Kinnerton Street, Belgravia, Westminster, London SW1X 8ED. Tel: 020 7235 1135. Monday to Saturday 11a.m.–11p.m. Sunday 12p.m.–10.30p.m. Food times Monday to Sunday 12p.m.–9p.m. Tube: Knightsbridge or Hyde Park Corner.

The Nag's Head is a 6–7 minute walk from Knightsbridge underground station, or a 10 minute walk from Hyde Park Corner.

This is the only other London pub to mount a challenge to the Pembroke/Coleherne as a nexus of death, this time for heterosexual killers.

In a bizarre and inexplicable coincidence, serial killer John Haigh used to frequent the very same pub as double killers Neville Heath and Donald Hume. All used to stand, at different times, in the same spot at the bar here.

The wooden-panelled pub is still here, with the same name, and is completely ordinary (apart from having a somewhat eccentric landlord who some people love and others dislike because he refuses to allow people to use mobile phones in his pub).

2) Jurys South Kensington Hotel (formerly Onslow Court Hotel)

109–113 Queens Gate, South Kensington. Tube: South Kensington.

Travel to South Kensington underground station. Leave the station via the exit. You are on Pelham Street. Walk to the right for a few seconds before crossing the road. You are now on Old Brompton Road. Walk down Old Brompton Road and in about 7–8 minutes you will come to a street called Queens Gate on the right and the hotel is on the right hand side. When Haigh lived at this hotel his Room number was 404 (although don't try and go up!)

Right around the corner is Manson Place!

> *'One may smile, and smile, and be a villain.'*
>
> **William Shakespeare, Hamlet**

> *'How can you prove a murder if there is no body?'*
>
> **John George Haigh**

Born in 1909, John Haigh is the second child in this book to have been born to strict Plymouth Brethren parents (Aleister Crowley being the first).

Haigh's parents set themselves apart believing that they were socially and spiritually superior to other people and they would not let their son John play with other children, or have friends come to the house. Haigh inherited or developed their superiority complex. Near the end of his life he had to share a cell with two other prisoners and he wrote to his parents 'I have no desire for protracted conversation below my intellectual level'.

Haigh learned to lie early and to lie often because everything he really wanted to do in life was frowned on by his disapproving parents. He became a consummate liar.

As an adult John Haigh did not look like some kind of mad-eyed, dishevelled, twitching maniac: he looked more like a sleekly successful door to door seller of, say, vacuum cleaners. With his Brylcreemed hair, little moustache and his vanity about his dapper appearance, he was the sort of man whom people would have called a 'spiv', that is to say someone a bit shallow, 'on the make', dishonest but charming – but not essentially a bad person.

The only thing noticeable about Haigh physically was a certain mask-like quality to his features and maybe a certain pallor. His brylcreamed hair and moustache lent him a resemblance (perhaps deliberately fostered) to notorious German serial killer Peter Kurten who had terrorised Dusseldorf 40 years before and whom Haigh would certainly have been aware of. Kurten was charged with killing nine people (the figure Haigh also claimed although there was no proof beyond six). Kurten claimed to be a vampire and Haigh too would advance a vampire motive for his murders claiming that he drank a glass of blood from each of his victims.

Haigh began with fraud and theft and had been jailed three times by the time he graduated to murder. He carefully studied chemistry and the law while in prison and carried out some little experiments on using acid to dissolve dead creatures. This shows premeditation when you consider the acid baths he later prepared for the human victims. His purchase of an industrial mincer to try to get rid of residual bits and pieces after the acid baths also shows extreme cunning and premeditation.

Haigh was almost pathologically cheerful. He was hardly ever seen without a smile on his face (probably even when the noose snaked around his neck, shortly to break it). He was a charming, courteous and correct chap most of the time, except when he was battering or shooting victims in the head, in a killing frenzy.

He was especially gentlemanly and honourable with girlfriends; in fact he seemed strangely disinterested in their physical attractions.

When he was 34, Haigh was squiring a 16-year-old schoolgirl, Barbra Stephens, who became the main woman in his life, and he behaved with perfect propriety towards her. She was probably useful cover (Kurten was married), and perhaps he was fascinated by her genuine innocence.

Stephens once had a dreadful nightmare in which Haigh drew a gun and shot someone – she later found out that the nightmare happened at the same time as the last victim Durand-Deacon was murdered by Haigh.

In his ordinary non-killing life Haigh suppressed his psychopathic 'Hyde' side amazingly well. Reading his letters to his parents is a strange experience. The letters are very revealing in what Haigh doesn't say. He never actually drops the mask of normality and liberally quotes from the Bible, which he clearly knows inside out from his formative years. However, if you read between the lines, he is actually continually goading and wounding the prim parents who helped make him a monster, 'It isn't everybody who can create more sensation than a film star, you know'.

Here is Haigh writing to his parents about fires when he was a fire-warden in the Second World War.

> *'I remember the fires during the war. I always thought it a pity they had to be put out; they always fascinated me.'*

A fascination with watching and setting fires is common among serial killers and one of the 'triad' of warning signs along with bedwetting and animal torture. Haigh's animal experiments have been noted earlier: the serial killer 'triad' was only identified by J.M. Macdonald in 1963.

Haigh's first victim (as far as is known) was 34-year-old Donald McSwan on 4 September 1944. Unlucky McSwan, whose parents had employed Haigh a few years earlier, had started socialising with Haigh again after accidentally meeting him in a pub.

Haigh took McSwan to some premises he was renting, battered him to death with a table leg and then dissolved him in acid. After fleecing them for money by pretending to be their son, and then concocting an excuse for them to visit, he utterly callously killed both McSwan's parents in the same room as he had killed their son. They were also dissolved in acid and flushed down the drain.

Haigh afterwards wore the dad's gold-rimmed spectacles, probably deriving pleasure from the secret flaunting of the trophy of a victim. Trophy-taking is a very common behavioural characteristic of serial killers.

Later he killed Archie and Rosalie Henderson, a couple he had stayed in touch with after enquiring about their house for sale, although he never bought it. He enjoyed playing the piano for them and they had a great time together until he killed them. Haigh had three great loves: music, money and murder.

He claimed to have killed two other men and a woman and dissolved them in acid too but no evidence was found. On the other hand a never-identified armless body was found at the foot of Beachy Head alongside a car Haigh had stolen. Haigh used to sit in his car at the top of Beachy Head with Barbra Stephens – it would be interesting to know what thoughts went through his head on those occasions.

His last certain victim was 69-year-old Olive Durand-Deacon who like Haigh was also living at the Onslow Court Hotel at the time. Haigh shot her in the head and then tried to dissolve her in acid, but he was only only partially successful on this occasion since her dentures were found, part of a female hip bone, her handbag handle, and some other bits and pieces, all of which led to his arrest.

After the arrest Haigh told the police:

> *'If I tell you the truth, you would not believe it. It sounds too fantastic.'*

At the trial Haigh claimed that he drained a cup of blood from each of his victims and had recurring vivid dreams about forests of blood-dripping crosses. Was this just shtick to make him seem insane so he would have an easier time in a mental hospital rather than in a prison? It's tempting to think so; after all Haigh himself was clearly aware of the merits of mental hospitals compared with prisons and had asked a policeman after his arrest, 'Tell me, frankly, what are the chances of anyone being released from Broadmoor?', Broadmoor being a rather notorious British mental hospital.

Nevertheless, the claims of blood-drinking may have been true, as they were in the case of Peter Kurten and a blood-stained pen-knife was found in his car. Haigh may have consciously tried to emulate Kurten, or perhaps he just knew that they were the same (perverse) breed.

In a letter to his parents he says enigmatically, 'There is a power outside oneself, which leads one on and on and to drink of the river of life is to experience more completely the fulness of life'. This sounds a lot like Renfield, Dracula's blood-drinking sidekick.

Haigh claimed his blood fixation began when he was a boy and his parents would punish him for wrongdoing by striking him with hairbrushes, drawing blood. He said he would lick his blood after those beatings and the fixation began. In due course, he says, he became obsessed with the bleeding Christ in the cathedral where he was a choirboy. A schoolgirl in his class claimed that while he was still a schoolboy Haigh threw her jacket on the train-track and told her, 'There is an express coming and it will run you over and cut you into little pieces and there will be blood all over the place'.

Haigh's killing of mainly older people is interesting. Many killers, even vicious ones, instinctively recoil from killing older people, presumably because they resemble one's parents or grandparents. Even the murderous and unscrupulous Lady Macbeth in Shakespeare's play *Macbeth* can't bring herself to kill King Duncan because he resembles her father. Haigh had no such compunction. The average age of his victims was 55.

Who was Haigh really killing by proxy when he murdered these older females and males? Probably his parents. The parents of whom he wrote from prison 'my recollection is of my father saying "Do not" or "thy shalt not" ... There was only condemnation and prohibition ... It is true to say that I was nurtured on Bible stories but those were mostly concerned with sacrifice.'

Haigh was hanged on 6 August 1949 by Albert Pierrepoint. Pierrepoint used his special strap to bind his wrists – he used this strap for people he particularly wanted to remember (the implication being because he found them so distasteful).

Haigh, like many serial killers, was a loner and a liar, colossally arrogant and vain and incapable of either pity or remorse. The last victim, the elderly Deacon-Durand, was merely 'a confounded nuisance ... she simply would not disappear'.

3) Millbank Prison

Tube: Pimlico.

There is a remembrance plaque for the prison on a bollard. To find the bollard, travel to Pimlico underground station. Use the Rampayne street exit on the left. Walk outside and turn right into Rampayne Street. In a few minutes you come to Vauxhall Bridge Road. Turn right into that road and walk for 5–6 minutes or so until you are approaching the river Thames, at which point the road changes name to Bessborough Gardens. Then cross over and walk down the road called Millbank and very soon on the left you will find a pub called the Morpeth arms, a good place for a drink. The Morpeth arms has a very unusual feature: live pictures transmitted from its cellars which the pub claims are haunted cells from Millbank prison. I am not convinced – they allowed me down there as a one-off and they felt and looked like arched storage spaces for kegs to me.

Right opposite the pub you will see a small, triangular-shaped park by the river wall. Walk through this park and at the end you will see a piece of modern art on a plinth. Just beyond is the bollard.

The inscription on the bollard says:

> *'Near this site stood Millbank Prison which was opened in 1816 and closed in 1890. This buttress stood at the head of the river steps from which, until 1867, prisoners sentenced to transportation embarked on their journey to Australia'.*

WATER, SOLITUDE AND THE LASH

Millbank was a holding prison for prisoners before they were transported, usually to Australia. Before transportation began to be used as a punishment the prisoners who ended up at Millbank would have likely been executed so they were often tough customers.

Millbank was an atypical prison in many ways, not least because prisoners tended to move on from it to their ships in a matter of months rather than stay for years on end (as would have been the case at Newgate for example.)

The origins of Millbank Prison go back to 1787 when the philosopher Jeremy Bentham wrote a chillingly efficient book called *The Panopticon* in which he proposed a new, 'better' system of prison architecture. Essentially Bentham proposed that prisoners be kept in a series of cells around the circumference of a circle at the centre of which would be constructed a tower containing an inspector who could then constantly survey the prisoners while remaining hidden himself.

Bentham was an ultra-rationalist and paid no attention whatsoever in his plan to the possible effects on the minds of his prisoners of constant isolation from each other, constant silence, and constant surveillance.

This Kafakesque system became the basis of Millbank prison although Bentham's system was never actually followed to the letter. For example, the six radiating wings of Millbank Prison as constructed look more like a snowflake.

The so-called perfect prison turned out to be an unworkable, flawed, expensive disaster. Even the location was bad since being close to the river there was damp unhealthy air.

Millbank started off as a prison conducted on the 'separate' system. Prisoners worked and slept alone and were not allowed to meet other prisoners. By the mid 1840s the prison had 1,100 separate cells. However the separate system (like the silent system in other prisons) was later abandoned at Millbank due to 'a distressing increase in the number of insane prisoners'. Fifteen prisoners had become insane. After the system was modified so that the prisoners were kept separate for the first 3 months, 'only five' became insane.

To travel forward in time for a paragraph before resuming our Millbank story, in the USA in 1971 a psychological experiment took place which became a classic. It was known as 'The Stanford Prison Experiment'. In the experiment volunteers were arbitrarily divided into two groups: prisoners and guards, for what was meant to be a two week study of what would happen in a pretend prison. The experiment showed that two things tended to happen – 'guards' tended over time to become more heartless and cynical towards the 'prisoners' in their charge, even sometimes to the point of sadism, while 'prisoners' tended to become more desperate, helpless and passive. The experiment had to be terminated early because it was getting out of control.

Events at Millbank when the governor in charge was a certain ex-military man named Captain John R. Groves, illustrate these tendencies well. The nature of the draconian system here was eventually raised in Parliament when a whistleblower guard quit and raised the alarm about abuses and suicides in the 3½ years he had worked there. Four prisoners had committed suicide in that time and another 12 had attempted it.

For example, one prisoner with a history of fits was ordered by Groves not to 'do any more of these tricks' and sentenced to three days on bread and water. Other prisoners were given seven days on bread and water although three days was the legal maximum. The governor would then sometimes give one day's ordinary food before putting prisoners back on the bread and water punishment regime.

The conscience-stricken guard also reported that Groves delighted in flogging prisoners with a specially constructed cat o' nine tails with double-sized thongs waxed at the ends to inflict more pain. He also enjoyed forcing the prisoners into the exercise yard on freezing cold days to 'test the fire drill' – the guard noticed that Groves seemed to enjoy doing this for the enjoyment of his friends.

Perhaps the biggest indictment of this brutal regime is the story of what happened to James Richmond, a boy of ten committed to the prison. Sometimes statistics overwhelm and make the mind shut down whereas information about the life and death of a single individual tells you more.

James Richmond was a 10-year-old Scottish boy who arrived at Millbank on 24 November 1845. Less than 6 months later, he died in the prison hospital. In that time he had been punished twelve times by having only bread to eat and water to drink, and less than 2 months before dying the final punishment had been ratcheted up to three days in the dark cell with only bread and water. In total during his 5 months in Millbank he'd been on bread and water for 22 days.

What had he done to deserve these punishments? On different occasions, his cell had been 'dirty', he'd broken the handle of his tankard, he'd been 'impertinent', he'd been 'marking his dinner tin'.

Being punished by having to stay in a solitary cell with no bed, just boards and a rug and a blanket was bad enough, but the dark cell, which Richmond suffered for three days and three nights before his death and which probably destroyed him, was a quantum leap worse.

The dark cell was in the bowels of the prison and was tiny with no furniture whatsoever and utterly without light. A writer was once shut up in Newgate's dark cell by a warder as a joke and he described it in the following terms 'Just about as near to being buried alive as you can possibly imagine ... the silence of the grave ... a living tomb ... my pulses were throbbing and my head seemed ready to burst ... I could endure no more'. When he was released he asked the warder how long he had been confined and was told 'Just three minutes!'

Groves thought it fit to confine 10-year-old James Richmond in there for 72 hours.

Even James was four years older than another Millbank prisoner, a 6-year-old boy who was sentenced to transportation 'and the sentence carried out into effect too, though the poor child couldn't speak plain' (warder to writer Henry Mayhew).

FIVE HORROR WRITER MEMORIALS (AND ONE MONSTER)

Mary Shelley, 24 Chester Square, SW1

One night in 1803 a grotesque and frightening scene took place in London. A scientist called Giovanni Aldini tried to reanimate a dead convict called George Forster using an electrical current and electrodes. 'On the first application of the process to the face, the jaw of the deceased began to quiver, and the adjoining muscles were horribly contorted, and one eye actually opened. In the subsequent course of the experiment, the right hand was raised and clenched, and the legs and thighs were set in motion; and it appeared to all the bystanders that the wretched man was on the point of being restored to life'.

The scene was so horrible that one witness who had accidentally been struck by the corpse's flailing right hand died of the shock a couple of days later.

This attempted reanimation incident can be said to have inspired the birth of Frankenstein on a wet night in 1816 at the Swiss Villa Diodati when Byron, Mary Shelley, Percy Shelley and John Polidori, along with Clare Clairmont, decided on a whim to write horror stories.

Eighteen-year-old Mary Shelley knew of the Aldini incident and in her novel she prominently featured the bringing to life of a corpse by electricity. 'I saw the hideous phantasm of a man stretched out, and then, on the working of some powerful engine, show signs of life, and stir with an uneasy, half vital motion...' (Introduction to the 1831 edition of Frankenstein)

There have been at least 3,000 spin offs from Mary Shelley's novel – films, tv shows, puppets, comics, ballets, etc.

Bram Stoker plaque, 18 St Leonards Terrace, Chelsea, SW3

Bram Stoker wrote Dracula here.

Bram Stoker was an Irish-born theatre manager who looked after actor Henry Irving's affairs for 27 years. The title character Dracula was partially based on Henry Irving at his most darkly brilliant and mesmeric. In fact Irving has been described as a 'psychic vampire' holding others in thrall to his personality. Irving had played the diabolical Mephistopheles. Abraham Van Helsing (Dracula's nemesis and eventual destroyer), is of course, Abraham (Bram) Stoker himself.

I have been to the crypt of St Michan's in Dublin which also had a part in Dracula's gestation (Stoker knew of its macabre contents). The crypt contains various skeletons including four in unlidded coffins. Bizarrely, due to the extremely dry air in the crypt which itself has something to do with local soil chemistry, the bodies in the four opened coffins are only partly skeletonised and they still have most of their skin. One skeleton is known as the 'Crusader' and crypt visitors are allowed to shake his finger. When I was a 12-year-old boy, one memorable day I did this. I remember the skeleton's bony hand was totally shiny due to thousands of people having shaken it.

Lord Byron statue, Hamilton Gardens, Hyde Park Corner, near statue of Achilles

By Lake Geneva on that famous stormy night in 1816 Byron could only produce a fragment of a vampire story, simply called 'A Fragment' and it was only a few pages long – but an entire literary genre had been created since it was the first vampire story in English history.

Polidori plaque, 38 Great Pulteney Street

Polidori, Byron's doctor, was the wild card on the famous night at Villa Diodati in 1816 when Frankenstein was conceived. Byron's fragmentary vampire story that night inspired Polidori to write something spooky himself and he came up with The Vampyre which is clearly an influence on Bram Stoker's Dracula. Polidori's suave but dastardly villain, Lord Ruthven, is partially based on Byron himself.

Robert Louis Stephenson, Abernethy House, Mount Vernon, NW3

Robert Louis Stephenson wrote Dr Jekyll and Mr Hyde in 1886. When actor Richard Mansfield put it on at the Lyceum Theatre in London in 1888, his transformation into Mr Hyde so frightened the audiences that a rumour began that Mansfield might be behind the Jack the Ripper murders terrorising the East End that autumn, and the play's run came to an abrupt end.

And one monster

Boris Karloff, real name William Henry Pratt (actor of Frankenstein's iconic anvil-headed monster) – plaque at 36 Forest Hill Road, East Dulwich, SE23.

7 SOUTH-EAST LONDON

1) Cross Bones: cemetery for medieval prostitutes

Cross Bones Graveyard, Redcross Way, London SE1. Website: www.crossbones. org.uk. Tube: Borough.

Travel to Borough on the Northern line and exit the station. Turn left, cross the road, and after about 5 minutes' walking on Borough High Street, turn left down Union Street and then right into Redcross Way. The Boot and Flogger pub is opposite the cemetery entrance.

THE OUTCAST DEAD

In Southwark in south London, close to a railway bridge in a location that you would think twice about visiting at night-time, is a shrine of sorts at a gate.

A drab locale has been transformed into a fantastic riot of colours and textures. There are poems, ribbons, flowers, tokens etc tied to the gate railings. There is also a bronze plaque stating 'The Outcast Dead R.I.P'. This is one of the most amazing places in London, a true underground phenomenon.

The writings fluttering here in the breeze reveal an outpouring of sympathy and respect for the poor and downtrodden prostitute women who were buried here in Shakespeare's time, and also for the paupers who were buried here in the Victorian era until the place was closed down, like so many other London graveyards, in the 1850s.

In medieval times Southwark was a disreputable place. It was south of the Thames and south of heaven. Theatres were built here, bears were killed here, and prostitutes conducted business here. At that time, strange as it may seem to modern sensibilities, the Catholic Church ran the prostitutes and the Bishop of Winchester was the ultimate beneficiary of the women's exertions. The prostitute women were therefore known as 'Winchester geese'. The use of the word geese was deliberately ambivalent since it had two meanings:

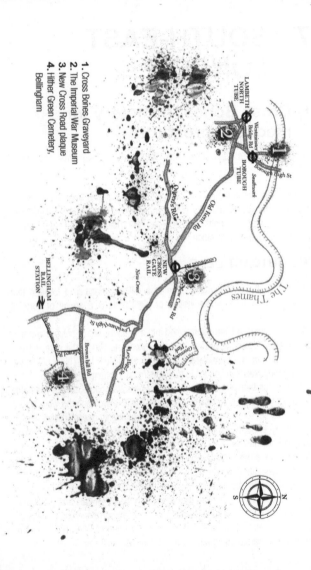

1. Cross Bones Graveyard
2. The Imperial War Museum
3. New Cross Road plaque
4. Hither Green Cemetery,
   Bellingham

LAMBETH NORTH TUBE

Westminster Bridge Rd

Southwark

BOROUGH TUBE

Borough High St

Queens Rd

Old Kent Rd

NEW CROSS GATE RAIL

New Cross

New Cross Rd

Woodpecker Rd

Greenwich Park

The Thames

BELLINGHAM RAIL STATION

Lewisham High St

Rushey Green

Brown hill Rd

Stanstead Rd

N
S

1) the bird we know as goose
2) a goose was also a swelling caused by sexual disease.

The first reference to this place is in historian John Stow's *Survey of London* where he euphemistically calls it 'The single woman's burial ground'. It was an unconsecrated place. The women who were deposited here had tough lives and most would have died young, at a time when people died young anyhow. Many would have died of diseases such as syphilis.

It is really not possible to talk about the Cross Bones Cemetery without giving a tip of the hat to poet/shaman John Constable, who has done more than anyone else to raise awareness of this place.

Constable has always had a keen sympathy for the outsider, feeling himself to be one, and one night in 1996 he had a strange dream visitation by a medieval prostitute. At one point she mentioned the phrase 'Cross Bones graveyard'.

Some time later reading a book he discovered by accident that, although it had been largely forgotten, there really was such a place, nor far from him in modern day Redcross Way, SE1.

Since his dream visitation Constable has devoted much of his time to talking and writing about this place and the lives of the women who lie here. As a direct result of his dream, many thousands of women, and many men too, have paid and continue to pay their respects at the site using the flowers, poems, etc mentioned earlier.

Modern day sex workers too also often come here to commemorate both the ancient dead who worked in their occupation, as well as more modern dead, including victims of serial killers. There are writings here, for example commemorating the five prostitute victims of the Ipswich serial killer in 2006.

It is a special place, one of London's best hidden places, and a necessary corrective to the glitz and glamour attached to so many other places in London where, effectively, money and social exclusion are celebrated.

The Museum of London did a small excavation here in the 1990s and found 160 skeletons but they estimated that was just 1% of the total, so there may be 15,000–16,000 people here. However that number would include both the poor people and the prostitutes buried indiscriminately here, together in death.

The site behind the gate is currently owned by Transport for London who want to develop it, but Constable and the friends of Cross Bones think a small garden of remembrance is the least that should be done to remember the dead here.

There is a hex or curse in place should that not happen.

2) Imperial War Museum (formerly Bethlem Hospital)

Lambeth Road, London, SE1 6HZ. Tel: 020 7416 5320. Open daily: 10a.m.–6p.m. Admission is free. Tube: Lambeth North.

Travel to Lambeth North underground station. Walk outside the only exit, cross at the lights and turn left into Westminster Bridge Road. Walk for about 8 minutes, staying on the right hand side. The road becomes St. George's Road. You will come to a crossroads with a Cathedral on your left called St George's. Cross over at the lights ahead of you and head for the distinctive green dome in view, underneath which is the main entrance.

I suggest sitting in the grounds when reading this chapter.

NOT LIKE US

'It is not always easy to distinguish between the keepers and the patients, in going around.'

Secretary to the commissioners for the regulation of madhouses, May 1815

Today the Imperial War Museum is based in the remaining central section of the 1815 building that once housed the third incarnation of the world's best-known lunatic asylum, Bethlehem Royal Hospital or Bethlem (or as it became popularly known, Bedlam). The striking dome originally held Bethlem's chapel.

The original Bethlehem dated back to 1247, and was where Liverpool Street Station is today. It began to specialise in the treatment of the insane in the fourteenth century and its fame spread to the point where the word Bedlam, a corruption of the original word, became synonymous with *any* lunatic asylum, particularly a chaotic and mismanaged one – a madhouse. This is analogous to the way that all prisons now are known as clinks from the name of London's original prison, The Clink.

In 1676, Charles II's reign, Bethlem No. 2 moved to a new building in Moorfields, a marshy area beyond the original city wall. The phrase 'out of sight, out of mind' comes to mind.

Until 1770 there were no restrictions on visitors, and the patients, who were often manacled or chained to the walls, were unwilling (and sometimes unwitting) public attractions. People would go for a day's outing, often on a Sunday, much as you might go to a zoo, to 'look at the funny lunatics'.

A famous painting, William Hogarth's 'The Rakes's Progress, Plate VIII' paint-ed in the 1730s and added to in the 1760s, gives some idea of the wretched-ness of life for patients in Bethlem at this point in its history. It shows patients in despair, or grinning or slumped, visitors slumming, etc.

When the old building became dangerously unstable it was decided to move to a new site in St George's Fields, Southwark where the Imperial War Museum is today. This was probably also an attempt to escape the bad publicity attached to the old site since the men's section there had been described as having 'the complete appearance of a dog-kennel'.

The campaigning of prison reformers such as John Howard, meant that more and more ordinary people had become uneasy at the conditions in which mentally ill people were being kept, and at the treatments being meted out to them. For example, an early form of electric shock treatment was being given at Bethlem from 1796 and in 1804 four patients had been strapped into a machine which then whirled them around one hundred times a minute!

The king himself at the time, George III, acted as an inescapable reminder that mental illness could strike anyone, even the greatest in the land, since he was himself severely mentally ill.

In August, 1815 122 patients (slightly more women than men) passed through the entrance hall, past two statues, 'raving' and 'melancholy madness', to get to their new accommodation. There was also a criminally insane section where patients would receive a complete change of straw about once a week. Louis Wain, who became famous for his paintings of cats, was in this section.

This new Lambeth-based Bethlem was meant to be a kindlier place than the other two incarnations had been and it is true that there were no chair-whizzings, whippings were out, and inmates were to be allowed outdoor exercise. It was downright cruel though not to put windows in the upper storeys of the new building (in wintertime!) because the authorities wanted to get rid of 'the disagreeable effluvias (smells) peculiar to all madhouses'. After complaints, glass was reluctantly installed the following summer; it is obvious that the mind-set was that mentally ill people didn't really feel anything like 'normal' people and therefore deserved to be treated like animals.

In fact in 1815, as Thomas Monro the man in charge admitted, the hospital's regime still consisted largely of 'bleeding, purging and vomiting.'

The Monro clan (they had a monopoly of the 'visiting physician' role for 125 years) came out of the 1815 enquiry very badly. Thomas Monro had rarely vis-ited the hospital and appears casual to the point of indifference in his replies to the committee. Here he is being asked about the bathing facilities for the patients:

> [Committee member to Monro]: 'Are they not all bathed together, immersed in water?'

> [Monro]: ' We have not ordered the bathing for some time, because the bath is in a very awkward place; ever since they took down the other part of the hospital, the bath is only in a situation where the men can go, therefore the women have not bathed'. (author's italics)

Thomas Monroe was not re-elected to his post in 1816. However his son took over instead (and then in turn, his son).

When the Monro reign ended, Dr Charles Hood took over in 1852 as the first resident physician. There were immediate humane improvements such as enlarged windows, aviaries, pictures, flowers, animals etc. Hood also immediately discontinued any mechanical form of restraint such as cuffs, straitjackets etc.

Once you were in Bedlam, particularly in the early years, it was very hard to get back out, 'We have no power of liberation [of a patient regaining sanity] under the Act'.

So there was a catch-22, the hospital was for treatment of insane people but if the treatment worked and a patient regained sanity they were not allowed back out, thereby presumably becoming insane again!

3) New Cross V-2 Woolworths bomb slaughter

277-281 New Cross Road. Nearest station: New Cross Gate.

Travel to New Cross Gate railway station (you can connect with the Underground system at Highbury and Islington). Leave the station, turn left and in about 3 minutes you will come to the Iceland Store, just after Goodwood Road, at 277–281 New Cross Road. There are two small plaques on the store.

ROCKET HORROR

THE BACKGROUND

In the later part of the Second World War the V-1 (Vengeance Weapon 1) and V-2 rockets represented a new order of terror due to their increased destructive capabilities. At one point the government even drew up contingency plans to withdraw the entire London population.

THE V-1 FLYING BOMB

First fired by the Germans from France, then later from other occupied counties, the first V-1 fell in London on 13 June 1944 in Bethnal Green, killing six and bringing down a railway bridge. This signalled the beginning of a new kind of Blitz, one with pilotless planes.

One problem with the attempt to counter these bombs by shooting at them was that if they were successfully struck they could crash on sites in London with the possibility of causing huge damage and large numbers of fatalities.

Londoners quickly became familiar with the signature sounds of a V-1's 'death rattle' followed by a hold-your-breath silence as the rocket nose-dived, followed by a massive explosion.

The psychological effect was to tremendously increase people's sense of vulnerability and large numbers of people left London at this period (although most later returned).

However, a two-pronged strategy by the British government of employing both land-based guns and air-based fighters on the coast meant increasing success in targeting and then destroying the rockets. Amazingly, fighter pilots even learned to flip the missiles off target mid-air, using their airplane's wing.

Many of the V-1s that got as far as London undershot and fell in south London which therefore bore a disproportionate amount of the damage and casualties.

At the height of the missile attacks there were sometimes 100 missiles in a day heading for London. Overall about one in four was getting through to actually fall on London; the rest were either successfully destroyed, fell off target, blew up because of technical faults, etc.

On one particularly proud night for London's defenders, 28 August 1944, 97 rockets entered British air-space, but only four actually reached London.

When it got through, the V-1 tended to cause structural damage to a wide area. In Croydon, south London, for example, a massive three-quarters of the buildings suffered V-1 damage.

In total 10,500 V-1s were launched, 3,957 were neutralised, 3,531 reached England and 2,353 hit London; 6,184 people in London were killed by V-1s.

WORST V-1 INCIDENT

On Sunday 18 June 1944 189 people were killed or seriously injured while attending mass at Wellington Barracks.

The last V-1 fell on 29 March 1945.

THE V-2 ROCKET

When the Germans realised that the threat from the V-1 terror weapon was being neutralised by British defences, the V-2 was introduced. Wernher Von Braun was responsible; he later worked on the American moon landings, and with Disney as technical director on a few space-related films.

The V-2 was a 45 foot tall rocket, with a bigger nosecone than the V-1 ant it carried about a ton of explosive. It was the weight of a London bus and it was the first inter-continental ballistic missile.

The first V-2 rocket fell in Chiswick (west London) on 8 September 1944. That was the day after Herbert Morrison, the Home Secretary, had reported in parliament that the Battle of Britain was over and had been won.

On average only about two or three V-2s a day reached London. The main target was meant to be the government citadels at Whitehall but bombs falling as much as a mile away were classified as close misses.

V-2s, like V-1s, also disproportionately affected south and east London: areas such as Catford and Poplar for example suffered greatly.

Perhaps counter-intuitively, the V-2 was not as much feared as the V-1. The reasons were, firstly, the government felt it had to initially censor news about V-2 rocket impacts and casualties so as not to panic people. Secondly, fewer V-2 rockets hit London and each individual rocket tended to be both silent (unlike the V-1) and unobserved while in the sky, which meant that by the time it struck only the people at that spot knew of it and were affected by it. Again, although there might be more deaths when a V-2 hit, the geographical spread of the damage caused by a V-2 tended to be smaller than with the V-1 because the rocket was heavier and buried itself deeper on impact.

However, as with the V-1, there could still be major incidents and on 1 November 1944 two incidents in south London in Camberwell and Deptford killed or badly wounded over 120 people.

Ultimately though the real and more hopeful story about the V-2 campaign was that out of a total of 1,200 V-2 air-launched (as opposed to ground-launched) rockets, only 66 actually reached London.

The last V-2 bombs to hit London fell on 27 March 1945. The second to last one to hit London fell on Hughes Mansions in Vallance Road (incidentally Vallance Road was where the Krays' mum's house nicknamed Fort Vallance, had been), killing 131 people.

One government nightmare kept secret from Londoners until after the war was over was the possibility of a V-2 strike rupturing a tube train while it was under the Thames. Such an incident was more than theoretically possible and the resulting flooding could have caused literally thousands of deaths due to the large numbers of people who had taken to sleeping in tube stations at night-time.

V-2 Attacks ended on 14 January 1945 because the Nazis were running low on fuel.

A total of 1,115 V-2 rockets reached England of which 517 hit London; 2,754 Londoners were killed by V-2 bombs.

In total, 8,938 Londoners were killed by either V-1 or V-2 bombs.

WORST V-2 INCIDENTS

8 March 1945 – Smithfield – 110 killed.

27 March 1945 – Stepney – 131 dead.

And the incident commemorated by the plaques in this story, the incident with the most terrible death toll of all the V-weapon incidents...

On Saturday 25 November 1944 at 12.26p.m. the 251st V-2 rocket to be launched left an island near Belgium and ploughed into the popular haberdashery shop, Woolworths, in New Cross, south London causing utter carnage. The shop had been particularly full because word had got out that there were going to be 144 saucepans for sale. One hundred and sixty-eight people died in the disaster, 100 more were injured; 24 of the dead were never identified. In addition to those killed in the shop and the shop queue, there were many other deaths from the Co-op store next door, an army lorry and a No. 53 double decker bus, etc.

A wide area was strewn with debris and body parts and the clean-up operation took three days. Corrugated iron was placed over victims in the aftermath of the explosion.

---

4) Sandhurst School and Hither Green Cemetery

Sandhurst Junior School, Minard Road, London SE6 1NW. 0208 698 1846. admin@sandhurstjs.lewisham.sch.uk. Nearest station: Lewisham.

Travel to Lewisham railway station. The bus station is nearby. Get the 284 bus to Verdant Lane, which is where the cemetery is – it takes about 17 minutes from the station. Ask the bus driver to let you know when approaching the stop for Hither Green Cemetery. Once inside the main entrance turn right and make your way along the main pathway heading right. The monument is within sight of the crematorium and can be identified by the conjunction of a large willow tree nearby and, uniquely in the Cemetery, two small palm trees at the site. If you still have a problem locating it, the grave-diggers will help.

The monument itself is a fairly large low enclosure with the victims' names written every few inches on white bricks. The patch of cemetery earth enclosed by the memorial is the resting place for most of the children killed by the bombing and machine-gunning.

Other than the victims' names there appears to be no other background information.

After visiting the Monument, and perhaps looking at some of the other impressive funerary monuments (angels etc.) in the Cemetery, there is something else you can do. Go back out the main entrance of the Cemetery, cross the road and turn right. Soon you come to Hazelbank Road on the left. Walk up it, and about 4 roads up on the right is Minard Road. Sandhurst Junior School is in Minard Road, on the left, after approximately another 10 minutes walking. There are Memorial Gardens within the school grounds including plaques in memory of the dead, a sculpture and some benches for contemplation but please note that **you have to arrange to see these memorial gardens in advance**. Either ring, write or email the school - you can find the contact details above.

There is also a little stained glass window containing the date January 20th 1943, the day of the massacre. The back of that very simple stained glass window memorial can be seen from Ardgowran Road which is the next road up, parallel to Minard Road.

HE WAS WAVING

On Wednesday 20 January 1943 at 12.30p.m., Sandhurst school in Catford, south London, was a place of hope and laughter and childish high spirits.

Lunch was taking place and some of the older kids were so excited because in the afternoon they would be going to see *A Midsummer Night's Dream*. Only they never went because at 12.31p.m. the children and adults at Sandhurst school in Catford, south London, were suffering hell on earth.

A German fighter bomber airpane, A FW-190, seemingly on its own, came in very low and machine-gunned and bombed the school. The pilot was waving.

Thirty-eight children and six adults were slaughtered.

There is a photo on the internet of a policeman directing the rescue attempt amid the rubble – his own daughter attended the school and was killed in the bombing.

On the following Monday, in slight rain, and with a guard of honour, most of the dead were buried in the local Hither Green Cemetery. Thirty-one small white coffins and one larger one, one of the six teachers. The equivalent of a class together in death, as they spent time together in life.

I give all the names here to try to bring home fully the human dimensions of this tragedy and as a way of moving beyond just a generic stating of casualty figures.

2013 is the 70th anniversary of the tragedy.

BURIED AT HITHER GREEN CEMETERY		
Forename	Surname	Age
Malcolm Britton	**Alexander**	11
Olive Hilda	Asbury	12
Joan Elizabeth	Baker	12
Betty	Barley	15
Dennis Handford	Barnard	10
Ronald Edward	Barnard	9
Anne Rosemary	**Biddle**	5
Judith Maud	**Biddle**	5
Kathleen Myrtle	**Brazier**	13
Joyce Agnes	Brocklebank	11
Pauline	Carpenter	5
Margaret	Chivrall	12
Winifred Mary	Cornell	13
Pauline Mary	Davies	7
Eunice Joan	Davis	5
Anthony	Drummond	9
Janet Mary	**Dutnall**	5
Richard George	Fagan	9
Cyril Arthur	Glennon	6
Norman Frederick	Greenstreet	8
Norah Marie	Harrison	9
Iris May	Hobbs	15
Rodney Charles Ash	Jarrett	6
John Edward	Jones	10
Harriet Irene	Langdon	40

(Continued)

(Continued)

Forename	Surname	Age
Doreen Alice	**Lay**	6
Mary Rosina	O'Rourke	15 ½
Evelyn Joyce	Scholes	11
Pamela Eileen	Silmon	10
Clive Derek	Tennant	8
Doreen	Thorne	12
Edna	Towers	12

DIED IN THE INCIDENT BUT BURIED ELSEWHERE

Forename	Surname	Age		
Brenda Jean	**Alford**	5	Ladywell Cemetery	
Lorna Elizabeth	Alford	7	Ladywell Cemetery	
Ethel Jessie	Betts	53	Cremation	Teacher
Donald Victor	**Brewer**	10	Private burial at Hither Green Cemetery on 26th	
Virginia May	Carr	38	Ballyglen, Ireland	Teacher
Pamela May Joyce	Cooper	15	Private burial at Hither Green Cemetery on 27th	
Joan	**Day**	12		
Olive Ann Margaret	Deavin	15	Tillingham	
Sylvia May Ellen	Head	12	Private burial at Hither Green Cemetery on 27th	
Mary Frances	**Jukes**	38	St Mary's, Harrow	Teacher

| Gladys Maud | Knowelden | 51 | Cremation | Senior Mistress |
| Constance May | Taylor | 58 | Private burial at Hither Green Cemetery on 27th | Teacher |

Names in **bold** died in hospital. Thanks for allowing me to reproduce this table are due to Lewisham Local History and Archives Centre and the War Memorials Wiki at http://lewishamwarmemorials.wikidot.com.

In fact, there were two hells that day: the original hell experienced by the dead and wounded, and then the inevitable second excruciating hell of the parents and loved ones. As one person who was part of the rescue mission expressed it, 'Parents were going mad at Sandhurst Road'. The same person forcefully expressed an opinion that after what he saw on that day, for him there was no God.

A small glint of hope and laughter in the aftermath of the tragedy – the Queen visited some survivors at Lewisham hospital and brought them some highly exotic and much-sought after bananas. Four-year-old Elizabeth Taylor looked at her precious banana and asked, 'Do I have to eat it?'

THREE MORE NOTORIOUS LONDON SERIAL KILLERS

John Duffy

'He turned into a monster with scary, scary eyes.'

John Duffy's ex-wife

'He really did have the most cold, penetrating, "laser-like" stare I had ever seen.'

Detective Charles Farquahar.

John Duffy, known as the 'railway killer', raped 26 women in and out of London and killed one of his three murder victims in Hackney, north-east London.

Duffy was an ugly, small and wiry runt of a man, possessed of two piercingly malevolent icy blue eyes (variously described as 'drill' or 'laser') with more than a hint of Charles Manson and Peter Sutcliffe about them.

Duffy was tiny and unattractive and had few friends. A blunt assessment of him by a schoolmate was, 'No-one liked him'. He felt inadequate around women and built up a murderous resentment towards them especially when his marriage collapsed due to its childlessness, Duffy's moroseness, and his insistence on tying up his wife before he could have sex with her.

Duffy's modus operandi was to talk to each of his three female victims as they walked through badly lit and isolated railway stations (he knew them all from having been a carpenter for British Rail). Due to his small size and slimness, Duffy might not necessarily have seemed threatening at that point. However, he would then bring out a knife and threaten the woman, forcing her away from the station to a nearby lonely area he had previously reconnoitred. He would then tie the woman's hands behind her back, rape, beat and kill her.

His 'signature' included: using chat up lines; using a special restraint for the victim's hands; tying the hands behind the back in a praying position, thumbs together; garrotting the women by means of a combination of a strip of fabric and a stick to wind it ever tighter around their throats; sometimes using karate blows as part of the beating; and attempting to get rid of forensic evidence by wiping the victim (also by dumping one victim's body in a canal and attempting to burn the body of another one).

Duffy began raping in 1982, initially as part of a two-man woman-hating team who'd met at secondary school when they were 11 years old. The other man was David Mulcahy. When Duffy was eventually arrested for three murders and multiple rapes, he initially kept quiet about Mulcahy's involvement in 18 joint rapes in just one year.

The pair would drive around hunting for victims, heightening the anticipation by listening repeatedly to Michael Jackson's song 'Thriller'. After committing these joint rapes, Duffy appeared to become a lone operator.

At least four stressors can be identified when you look at the timeline of Duffy's actions. A stressor is something that happens in a serial killer or rapist's life that makes them feel especially angry, humiliated or frustrated and that prompts them into action.

1) He began to rape only weeks after being sacked from his job.
2) He stopped raping at a time when he and his wife attempted to repair their relationship but started a second wave of rapes when they broke up for good.
3) He had a lucky escape when a rape victim was too traumatised to be able to identify him in court; later that same month Duffy committed his first murder.

4) He killed for the last time one week after being stopped and questioned by two detectives working on the case.

Duffy was caught by a combination of three things: a mixture of good detective work (for example, a detective noticed that one of the rapes had various features in common with one of the murders), good use of the pooled computer databases the investigators had built up, and psychological profiling.

A Surrey professor of applied psychology, David Canter, was asked to take a look at the case. Looking at the common features Canter came up with a 17 point profile – it was later found that 13 of the points applied correctly to Duffy.

One technique Canter used, and which he is now an acknowledged expert in, was geographic profiling. This postulates that a rapist or serial killer will often commit their initial crimes close to their home area because they feel more comfortable there. Canter noted that rapes 1, 2 and 4 occurred close together and all close to Kilburn in north London. Canter correctly guessed therefore that the killer lived close to the Kilburn area. He also thought that the killer would be semi-skilled; probably married but with a bad relationship with his wife; interested in martial arts; a keeper of souvenirs from his crimes (Duffy had kept 33 keys from various victims), etc. When all 17 points were fed into the combined databases of two investigative teams, Duffy's name came out in seconds.

The judge who gave Duffy a 30 year prison sentence described him as a 'predatory animal'.

Ten years into the sentence, Duffy for some reason finally revealed he had had an accomplice and gave father of three David Mulcahy's name. Duffy broke down at this second trial and gave evidence that Mulcahy was present at all three murders and had taken the lead. Evidence did in fact emerge that Mulcahy had been the leader and had been even more violent towards the women than Duffy. David Mulcahy was also sent to prison for life.

Levi Bellfield

Bellfield (birth name Levi Rabetts) is a 6 foot 1 (1.8 metres), 20 stone (127 kg) steroid-taking, slug-like individual serving a life sentence for three murders.

His geographical comfort zone for attacks was the Twickenham area, west London.

Bellfield could not stay away from women – at the time of his arrest he was 36 years old and had already had 11 children with five different women – but although he could be superficially charming until they were under his control, he actually hated woman with a passion. He oozed misogyny. A girlfriend once found a series of magazines he had kept in which he had scratched out the faces of all the blonde women. Another of his girlfriends found a secret rape kit. He raped his girlfriends on many occasions and also regularly drugged with date-rape chemicals the drinks of girls he met when he was a bouncer for nightclubs. This was the perfect job for him as it gave him access to scores of vulnerable young women, often the worse for drink. He often took young girls to his van which he had equipped with carpet and handcuffs. He even bragged to a girlfriend that he had raped a disabled girl after lifting her from her wheelchair. The police believe he was responsible for many rapes in this way but it's impossible now to know the number because the drugged alcohol rendered the girls almost senseless and obliterated their memories.

Bellfield pursued petite woman who were in their early teenage years who he could impress and control more easily. 'He got off on rage and control', an ex-girlfriend said. The steroids he abused may possibly have played a part in the rages.

Many of his girlfriends ended up in nightmare relationships with Bellfield in which they were basically kept and used as sex slaves for years. One girlfriend said she would wet herself when she heard his key in the door. They knew better than to tell anyone though, if they wanted to avoid an even more brutal attack. One eventually cracked and did leave him to go to a woman's refuge with their children but he wormed his way back into her life.

He enjoyed having a harem of girlfriends but while obsessively jealous and controlling, he would at the same time constantly leave them without explanation and roam around at night-time using different cars.

The pattern of the abuse of his multiple, overlapping girlfriends – verbal abuse, punching, kicking, slapping, half-strangling, and raping at knifepoint – was so extreme and escalated to such a degree that it was almost inevitable that he would descend to murder.

His first murder was blonde 13-year-old Milly Dowler in March 2002. Her name will be familiar to many who read this book because the police hunt for her was so intensive and millions saw her elfin smiling face on their TV screens. Her murder had been one of the most high-profile and frustrating murder cases in recent years. She was snatched metres away from a house in Walton-on-Thames where Bellfield was staying at the time. We'll never know what he did to her; her skeleton, with no clothes anywhere nearby, was found 6 months later.

His second murder was 19-year-old Marsha McDonnell in February 2003, hit three times on the back of the head in Kingston, just 100 metres from her parents' house.

The third girl he murdered was French, Amelie Delagrange, in August 2004 on Twickenham Green. She was 22 when he snuffed her life out by smashing her head from behind.

Milly, Marsha, and Amelie. All young, blonde petite women. All complete strangers to Levi Bellfield but destroyed by him nevertheless.

His modus operandi for murder was to stalk the women from one of a variety of cars he owned, either as they waited at bus stops or as they travelled on late-night buses which meant that he could see through the bus windows that they were alone or almost alone.

In the case of buses he'd follow in the car until he saw the woman was getting off, then drive ahead, park the car and wait. When the woman walked ahead of him he would smash them on the back of the head from behind in a similar fashion to the way that Peter Sutcliffe, the Yorkshire Ripper, attacked his victims. The weapon was never found but was probably a hammer, again like Sutcliffe. Something like five other women around that area survived being attacked in this same way. It is very probable that Bellfield was responsible for some or all of those attacks but unless he confesses, which is very unlikely, we won't know.

Bellfield has been told by the authorities that he will never be released and will die in prison.

Kenneth Erskine

1n 1986, 24-year-old Kenneth Erskine, of no fixed abode, would routinely turn up on Mondays at a Stockwell government office to claim his emergency unemployment money. He was quiet, so quiet in fact that members of the staff there nicknamed him 'the whisperer' because of his strangely introverted, dissociated manner.

On Monday 28 July 1986 a team of police swooped at the office and led the grinning Erskine away, to be confirmed as the man police had been desperately hunting for, a man with a different, media-bestowed nickname, 'the Stockwell strangler'.

With a mental age of 10 but feral and cunning, Erskine was a severely disturbed individual who murdered at least seven old people. The murders were clustered around Stockwell in south London but three victims were killed further off. They had all been strangled with one hand. Unusually, the victims included both men and women (three women and four men) and most, of both sexes, had been sexually assaulted. The police believe it is very possible he killed other people whose deaths at the time were not recognised as murder.

The one survivor of an attack told how Erskine had jumped on his chest and squeezed his throat, then released, then squeezed again, then released, all the while repeating one word, 'Kill ... kill ... kill'.

Erskine was someone who had fallen through the cracks in society, a drifter, a wraith-like figure living for 8 years a hand-to-mouth existence in squats and God knows where else. When his photo was released by the police, not one person came forward to say that he was a friend, and no personal possessions of his were found.

What personal circumstances led him to want to attack defenceless old people whose average age was 80 is still not known since Erskine has apparently never talked about it. Was it connected to the fact that his family had kicked him out and stopped contact with him when he was 16 years old?

Four years before the murders when Erskine had been 20 years old and in prison for burglary he had painted pictures showing old people being knifed and burnt.

Although he told the police he wanted to be famous, it is hard to avoid the conclusion that at some time in his life Erskine felt he had been brutalised by somebody considerably older than himself and that he had been triggered by something into seeking revenge for this.

Erskine was imprisoned in 1988 and given a minimum prison sentence of 40 years.

In 1996 he came to the defence of fellow serial killer Peter Sutcliffe (the Yorkshire Ripper) when Sutcliffe was being attacked by other prisoners.

INDEX